VOICE and MOOD

Essentials *of* Biblical Greek Grammar

Stanley E. Porter, *series editor*

Voice and Mood: A Linguistic Approach
by David L. Mathewson

VOICE
and MOOD

A Linguistic Approach

DAVID L. MATHEWSON

Baker Academic

a division of Baker Publishing Group
Grand Rapids, Michigan

© 2021 by David L. Mathewson

Published by Baker Academic
a division of Baker Publishing Group
PO Box 6287, Grand Rapids, MI 49516-6287
www.bakeracademic.com

Printed in the United States of America

Library of Congress Cataloging-in-Publication Data
Names: Mathewson, David, author.
Title: Voice and mood : a linguistic approach / David L. Mathewson.
Description: Grand Rapids, Michigan : Baker Academic, a division of Baker
   Publishing Group, [2021] | Series: Essentials of biblical Greek grammar | Includes
   bibliographical references and indexes.
Identifiers: LCCN 2021011634 | ISBN 9781540961433 (paperback) | ISBN
   9781540964861 (casebound) | ISBN 9781493420520 (ebook)
Subjects: LCSH: Greek language, Biblical—Voice. | Greek language, Biblical—Mood. |
   Bible. New Testament—Language, style.
Classification: LCC PA847 .M34 2021 | DDC 487/.4—dc23
LC record available at https://lccn.loc.gov/2021011634

Unless otherwise indicated, Scripture translations are the author's own.

Unless otherwise indicated, quotations from the Greek New Testament come from Eberhard Nestle, Erwin Nestle, Barbara Aland, Kurt Aland, Johannes Karavidopoulos, Carlo M. Martini, and Bruce M. Metzger, eds. *Novum Testamentum Graece*. 28th rev. ed. Stuttgart: Deutsche Bibelgesellschaft, 2012.

21   22   23   24   25   26   27   7   6   5   4   3   2   1

CONTENTS

Series Preface   vii

Acknowledgments   ix

Introduction   1

PART 1 Voice

1. Recent Scholarship on Voice   7

2. Linguistic Model and Voice   25

3. The Three Voices in New Testament Greek   51

PART 2 Mood

4. Recent Scholarship and Linguistic Insights on Mood   77

5. The Greek Mood System   95

6. Infinitives and Participles   137

Conclusion   169

Bibliography   173

Author Index   181

Scripture Index   185

Subject Index   189

SERIES PREFACE

I am pleased to introduce the Essentials of Biblical Greek Grammar series. This new and innovative set of volumes is designed to introduce scholars, students, and others who are interested in recent developments in Greek language studies to some of the most important topics in current discussion. This series is accessible and suitable for use in the classroom and in research.

Current treatments of the Greek language of the New Testament still often slavishly employ the categories of traditional grammar, even though there have been monumental developments in linguistic studies throughout the last century. The last thirty or so years have seen significant interest in the study of New Testament Greek from a more linguistically informed perspective, and these volumes attempt to capture and reflect that interest. Each of the volumes is written by a scholar who has made a noteworthy contribution to the discussion of Greek grammar and linguistics and who has experience teaching such concepts. These books are not designed simply to reinforce or summarize the entrenched categories often used in Greek language studies, nor do they offer only theoretical discussions. Instead, they offer linguistically informed treatments of major topics—but without getting mired in technical, theoretical language. They are designed to introduce readers to the major areas of discussion, the pertinent issues within these areas, and suitable categories that are transferable from linguistics to Greek language description—and they provide enough examples to illustrate how these topics influence exegesis. Along the way, each volume offers new proposals on how to understand its respective topic and some new ways of exegeting that will have an impact on our understanding of the New Testament.

The books within this series address some of the fundamental topics in Greek language studies but also include topics more recently incorporated into Greek linguistics. One volume treats lexical semantics, showing approaches to Greek vocabulary and suitable ways of discussing words and their meanings. Another volume discusses Greek syntax, with attention to the ways that various groupings of words, such as sentences, are organized and with attention to their meanings. One of the volumes in this series addresses the functions of the Greek mood and voice systems, presenting the most recent points of contention while making a positive proposal regarding these two important yet often overlooked categories. Another volume is dedicated to discussion of Greek verbal aspect, defining what is meant by "aspect" and proposing a straightforward way of understanding this semantic category. There is also a volume on discourse analysis, which assumes many of the kinds of discussions found in other volumes within this series but brings them into conversation as a means of examining not just words, clauses, or individual components but an entire text and how it conveys its meaning.

Every serious reader of the Greek of the New Testament will benefit from this series and be able to incorporate these insights into their own exegetical work.

Stanley E. Porter
McMaster Divinity College

ACKNOWLEDGMENTS

Writing a book on Greek grammar these days requires being knowledgeable of the Greek language itself, while also being conversant with recent linguistic insights and how that should influence the approach to Greek grammar. The days should be past when Greek grammars are produced that do not rely on linguistic approaches. My first foray into the application of linguistics to the writing of a Greek grammar was Stanley E. Porter's *Verbal Aspect in the Greek of the New Testament*. It is now my privilege to contribute a volume to a series edited by Professor Porter. I have attempted to implement insights from a particular linguistic model that I find productive in thinking about grammar, which has been the focus of attention in much of Stan's work.

I am grateful to Stan for his confidence in me to contribute this volume to this series, and for his encouragement and interest in my ongoing work in Greek and linguistics. Lengthy conversations with him over email have enhanced this volume. I would also like to thank the Linguistics Circle at McMaster Divinity College (Hamilton, Ontario) for interacting with a presentation of much of the material in this book, and for their thoughtful and helpful comments on it. Lastly, the editorial staff at Baker Academic has been a delight to work with at all stages of the production of this work.

INTRODUCTION

Voice, Mood, and the Greek Verb System

At the center of the Greek clause stands the verb, which expresses the verbal process. It is the verb that communicates the "doings" and "happenings" within the discourse, moving the discourse forward and affecting the participants in the sentence in some way.[1] That is, a clause is primarily about the events or states in which the actors in the clause are involved or by which they are affected. The Greek verb is also the most semantically weighty element of the clause, contributing the meaningful features of aspect, voice, mood, person, and number. Therefore, an informed understanding of the Greek verb is of utmost importance for any exegesis of the Greek New Testament.

As a fusional (or inflectional) language, Greek indicates all these major features of its verbs—aspect, voice, mood, person, and number—through its "tense" endings,[2] which is why first-year Greek students spend so much time memorizing endings when they get to verbs (a change in any of these five features requires a change in the formal ending). In other words, these semantic features related to the

---

1. "The heart of the Greek language is the verb" (Decker, *Reading Koine Greek*, 217).
2. By using the terminology of "tense endings" or "tense forms" I am not implying that the verbal endings in Greek indicated true tense or time. I am only following standard terminology to identify the *morphological endings* on verbs that indicate the different semantic features of aspect, voice, mood, person, and number.

various grammatical functions of the verb are communicated morphologically by the selection of a given verbal ending from a system of choices (e.g., singularity vs. plurality, first person vs. second person, or perfective vs. imperfective aspect). This suggests that an important linguistic principle for interpreting the Greek verbal system (or any part of the grammatical system) is that "meaning implies choice," as the grammar can be seen as a series of meaningful choices within the language system.[3] This important linguistic notion will be developed further below. But as it applies to this volume the various semantic features of the verbal system must be considered in relationship to one another as choices from within a system (rather than examined in isolation, as most grammars do by treating the various features of verbs individualistically and discussing in isolation various functions). The purpose of this volume is to explore in some detail two of those features of the Greek verb system indicated by the verb endings that are important for interpreting the Greek New Testament: voice and mood.

Voice

Though probably not as semantically and exegetically significant as verbal aspect, voice is an important feature of the New Testament Greek verb system. Voice is indicated by the selection of a formal ending, which grammaticalizes semantically the relationship of the grammatical subject (not necessarily the agent) to the action of the verb. Most Greek grammars understand the voice system in this manner: "Voice relates the action to the subject."[4] However, a fruitful approach that is beginning to emerge among some discussion of verbal voice is to also interpret the Greek voice system more specifically as communicating the semantic feature of *causality*. That is, voice "is a semantic category by which a speaker/writer grammaticalizes a perspective on how a process is caused."[5] Is the action caused by an external agent, or is it internally caused? Therefore, voice considers how the subject

---

3. Mathewson and Emig, *Intermediate Greek Grammar*, 114.
4. Robertson, *Grammar of the Greek New Testament*, 798.
5. O'Donnell, *Corpus Linguistics*, 371. See also Porter, "Did Paul Baptize Himself?"

relates to the verbal process in terms of causality. This way of looking at the voice system in Greek will be developed in more detail below. Though the question of the number of voices in Greek persists, as will be argued in the ensuing discussion, the Greek language exhibits three separate voices based on morphology, but more importantly semantically based on causality: active, passive, and middle. Though the voice system would seem to be relatively straightforward and does not perhaps carry the same exegetical weight as the semantic feature of verbal aspect, or even probably the feature of mood,[6] study of the voice system in Greek is complicated by a number of factors. A few of these include the precise meaning and definition of the voices, the question whether Greek is a two- or three-voice system, the relationship between the voices semantically and systemically, the interpretive and exegetical significance of the voices, and the validity of the concept of "deponency" as it applies to certain verbs. These and other issues related to Greek voice will be considered in the discussion below. Though overshadowed by attention given to verbal aspect, the voice system in Greek has recently attracted some scholarly attention that has moved the discussion forward.

Mood

The semantic feature of mood is also important for understanding the Greek verb, and perhaps is second in importance to verbal aspect for interpreting Greek verbs. Unlike some languages, such as English, which indicate mood lexically through modal auxiliaries (e.g., "*would* study," "*could* study," "*might* study"), mood in the ancient Greek language is indicated, like aspect and voice, morphologically through the selection of a formal verb ending. Mood in Greek semantically indicates the author's attitude toward the action, or his or her view of the action as it relates to reality. Thus, "*the mood forms are used to grammaticalize the language user's perspective on the relationship of the verbal action to reality. . . .* The mood forms

6. This is apparent from the space devoted to the discussion of voice in Greek grammars, compared to the space given to the discussion of verbal aspect and even mood.

indicate the speaker's 'attitude' toward the event."[7] Scholars are usually careful to distinguish mood as indicating the author's attitudinal
perspective on the action from whether the action itself corresponds
to reality; it is the *author's perspective* on or *attitude* toward the relationship of the action to reality that is important, not the factual
status of the event.[8] There are four moods in the New Testament
Greek verbal system: indicative, subjunctive, optative, and imperative. They can be distinguished according to assertive (indicative) and
nonassertive (subjunctive, optative, imperative) semantics. Each of
these moods will be considered separately and in more detail below.
Once again, though not attracting nearly the attention that the Greek
verb aspectual system does, as indicated by the little substantial work
being done on mood outside of Greek grammars, there are a number of issues and factors that must be considered when discussing
the Greek mood system. These include the semantics of the moods,
the relationship of the moods systemically, linguistic approaches to
mood, the relation of the moods to speech roles, and the interpretive
significance of the moods. These and other issues related to mood
will be addressed in this volume. It will also briefly treat the possible
relationship between three other verbal forms and mood: the future,
infinitives, and participles.

Summary

The following chapters of this book will treat in some detail grammatical voice and mood in New Testament Greek. In each part recent research will be surveyed, the chosen linguistic model for our
investigation will also be articulated, and numerous examples will
be given to illustrate the value of the discussion for interpreting the
New Testament. The first part of this work will consider the New
Testament Greek voice system.

---

7. Porter, *Idioms*, 50. Italics his.
8. Mathewson and Emig, *Intermediate Greek Grammar*, 160; Wallace, *Greek
Grammar*, 445.

PART 1

VOICE

Recent Scholarship on Voice

Introduction

Voice is a significant but frequently underdeveloped feature of the Greek verbal system. Yet it can be very important for interpreting the Greek New Testament. To illustrate voice, the following two English sentences are semantically similar in their content and what they describe as taking place; they differ, however, in their perspective on the way the action is portrayed as taking place and how the participants are involved in or affected by the action within the clause:

The student purchased the book.
The book was purchased by the student.

In simple terms, in the first sentence the subject, "the student," is responsible for initiating the action of purchasing, with "book" being the object or recipient of the action. However, in the second sentence "the book" is now the grammatical subject, but it is still the recipient of the action of purchasing. In the second sentence the entity responsible for initiating the action of purchasing, the agent of the action ("student," which is the subject in the first sentence), is now indicated by the prepositional phrase "by the student." The grammatical feature that deals with this phenomenon is *voice*, specifically how the subject relates to the action of the verb. The former sentence is an example of an English active voice construction, and the latter a passive voice construction. As already noted, Greek indicates voice through the use of a series of verb endings. In addition to the active and passive voices illustrated in the above examples, Greek also exhibits a third voice not represented in English: the middle.

The first chapter of this section will consider contemporary treatment of voice in the Greek of the New Testament. It will discuss voice as it is explained in recent Greek grammars and then consider three specialized studies of voice in ancient and New Testament Greek. The next chapter will lay out the linguistic model followed in this part of the book on voice. I will argue that Systemic Functional Linguistics (SFL) provides a workable model for understanding the Greek voice system, once the difference between the voice system in Greek and English is understood. The third and final chapter of this section will consider the meaning of voice in Greek, followed by a treatment of each of the individual voices as well as deponency and the interpretive significance of voice.

Recent Treatments of Voice in New Testament Greek Grammars

Ancient Greeks referred to voice as διάθεσις (*diathesis*), referring to the disposition of the subject to the action of the verb.[1] Both ancient and modern grammars have theorized on the meaning and function of voice in the ancient Greek language. Here we will consider only some of the more recent attention given to the voice system in the Greek of the New Testament. The lack of attention to voice is beginning to be rectified with some important work on the Greek voice system (see below). In this first portion of this chapter we will consider the treatment of voice in intermediate-level and reference-type Greek grammars. Modern-day New Testament Greek grammars frequently treat voice in somewhat abbreviated fashion, often

---

1. Fletcher, "Voice in the Greek of the New Testament," 57; Lyons, *Theoretical Linguistics*, 372.

as part of a general introduction to the Greek verb or in connection
with other elements of the Greek verb (e.g., person and number),
and with little theoretical reflection on the voice system in Greek.[2]
Usually grammars include a very brief definition and discussion of
voice, followed by (with few exceptions) a fairly standard list of labels that ostensibly classify the variety of voice usages in context.
To illustrate the typical treatment of voice in Greek grammatical
discussion, we will consider and summarize only a selection of the
most recent grammars.

Stanley E. Porter, in his *Idioms of the Greek New Testament*,
defines voice as "a form-based semantic category used to describe
the role that the grammatical subject of a clause plays in relation to
an action."[3] Despite his rather informed treatment of Greek voice
covering eleven pages, Porter admits that there is much more work
to be done on voice in New Testament Greek. In his treatment of
the specific voices, Porter states that for the active voice "the agent
. . . is the grammatical subject of the verb."[4] In relationship to the
other voices, it is the least semantically weighty. He discusses the
active voice in relation to its use with verbs of perception, its use
with verbs of motion, and its usage with the accusative case functioning adverbially. For the passive voice, the grammatical subject
is the object or recipient of the verbal process, placing attention
on the grammatical subject as the recipient of the action. Porter
discusses the passive voice in relation to specified and unspecified
agency, and the role of the accusative case objects. Finally, the middle
voice, rather than carrying a reflexive meaning, expresses more direct
participation, specific involvement, or some form of benefit of the
grammatical subject.[5] The middle is the most semantically weighty
of the three voices. Rather than relying on the typical labels used by
other grammars (see below), Porter discusses translating the middle
voice, important usages in the New Testament, and the issue of

---

2. Köstenberger, Merkle, and Plummer give it only just over six pages of treatment
in a chapter overviewing Greek verbs (*Going Deeper with New Testament Greek*,
193–99). However, cf. Wallace, who gives voice thirty-five pages in a separate chapter
(*Greek Grammar*, 407–41).

3. Porter, *Idioms*, 62.

4. Porter, *Idioms*, 63.

5. Porter, *Idioms*, 67.

deponency. On deponency, Porter is ambiguous about its value and concludes that the interpreter might be justified in finding middle meaning in all deponent verbs.[6]

Richard A. Young devotes three and a half pages to voice.[7] He defines voice as "a morphological feature that conveys the relation of the subject to the action of the verb."[8] In general, the active voice means the subject performs the action, the middle voice indicates the subject participates in the results of the action, and the passive voice means the subject is the recipient of the action. He then proposes the following labels (a mixture of semantic and functional notions) for their various usages in context: active—simple, causative, reflexive; middle—direct (reflexive, which is rare), indirect, permissive, reciprocal, deponent; passive—thematizing the subject, omitting the agent, emphasizing the agent, passive with a middle sense, deponent passive. Deponent verbs, according to Young, have middle or passive forms but are active in meaning.[9]

In his important study on the Greek verb, Kenneth L. McKay devotes a separate chapter to voice, covering six pages.[10] His treatment of voice is from the perspective of the relationship of the grammatical subject to the action of the verb. McKay postulates three voices in Greek: active, passive, and middle. Basically, the active voice represents the subject as engaging in the action of the verb; the passive voice, the subject being acted upon; and the middle voice, the subject as acting on, for, or toward itself.[11] Because he sees it as differing little from its English counterpart, the active voice requires little explanation, though sometimes the active can be used when the agent has someone else act for him or her. For the middle voice, McKay says that it "is characterized by a reflexive idea"[12] and then reverts to some of the typical labels for describing its function in different contexts: reflexive, reciprocal, and causative. He also discusses its usage with transitive and intransitive verbs. The passive

6. Porter, *Idioms*, 72.
7. Young, *Intermediate New Testament Greek*, 133–36.
8. Young, *Intermediate New Testament Greek*, 133.
9. Young, *Intermediate New Testament Greek*, 135.
10. McKay, *New Syntax*, 21–26.
11. McKay, *New Syntax*, 21.
12. McKay, *New Syntax*, 21.

voice, according to McKay, apparently developed through the middle. McKay primarily discusses how agency with the passive voice is indicated. He also feels that passive forms do not always indicate passive meaning, and the form extends to more than the passive meaning. He ends his discussion of voice with a consideration of the issue of deponency, where he questions its necessity. Many verbs that are passive or middle deponent have a middle or passive element in their meaning or history.[13]

Daniel B. Wallace has the lengthiest and most detailed discussion of voice among Greek grammars, devoting an entire chapter of thirty-five pages to it.[14] His discussion is fairly typical of the way voice is usually treated. Unlike Porter, and as in most grammars, he describes the three voices not in relationship to each other but independently. He defines voice as the "property of the verb that indicates how the subject is related to the action (or state) expressed by the verb."[15] He then simplistically describes the voices as follows: the active voice indicates the subject doing the action, the passive voice indicates the subject as receiving the action, and in the middle voice the subject is both doing and receiving the action, a combination of both active and passive.[16] Furthermore, the middle voice "emphasizes the subject's participation" in the action.[17] That is, it appears that the only thing that distinguishes the active from the middle voice is more emphasis on the subject acting in the middle. Wallace also distinguishes voice from the category of transitivity (transitive vs. intransitive verbs). This is followed by a treatment of the three voices in terms of a full list of labels that capture their ostensible functions in various contexts: active voice—simple active, causative active, stative active, reflexive active; middle voice—direct (reflexive) middle (which Wallace thinks is rare), redundant middle, indirect middle, causative middle, permissive middle, reciprocal middle, deponent middle; passive voice—simple passive, causative/permissive passive, deponent passive. Wallace is cautious about the value of deponency

13. McKay, *New Syntax*, 25–26.
14. Wallace, *Greek Grammar*, 407–41.
15. Wallace, *Greek Grammar*, 408.
16. See Wallace's "directional" illustration (*Greek Grammar*, 409).
17. Wallace, *Greek Grammar*, 414.

for understanding verbs that possess only middle or passive forms, but he still sees some verbs as true deponents.[18]

In his more popularized intermediate-level grammar, David Alan Black treats voice in just over two pages in a chapter that provides an overview of Greek verb inflection.[19] Black defines the three voices in a simple manner: the active voice is where the subject produces the action; the passive voice is where the subject receives the action of the verb; and the middle voice stands in between, where the emphasis is on the subject as the agent of the action of the verb. The reflexive meaning of the middle has all but disappeared. He then appeals to the common labels and categories of usage found in most grammars. For the active: simple active and causative active. For the passive: simple passive and permissive passive; this is followed by a discussion of different types of agency that can be expressed with the passive voice: primary (personal), secondary (intermediate), and instrumental (impersonal). For the middle voice: direct (reflexive), intensive, and reciprocal. He also finds a number of deponent verbs, which have middle or passive endings but are active in meaning.

In their intermediate grammar *Going Deeper with New Testament Greek*, Andreas Köstenberger, Benjamin Merkle, and Robert Plummer treat verbal voice in only six pages, and as part of a chapter on a general introduction to Greek verbs.[20] They offer a fairly standard definition of voice: "The voice of the verb indicates the way in which the subject relates to the action or state expressed by the verb."[21] They likewise offer a brief description of each voice in terms of whether the subject performs the action (active), participates in the results of the action (middle), or receives the action (passive). This is followed by a list of repeated, common labels of usages for each voice: active—simple, causative, reflexive; middle—reflexive, special interest, permissive (causative), deponent; passive—simple, permissive, deponent.

18. See Wallace's list in *Greek Grammar*, 430.
19. Black, *Still Greek to Me*, 93–96.
20. Köstenberger, Merkle, and Plummer, *Going Deeper with New Testament Greek*, 193–99.
21. Köstenberger, Merkle, and Plummer, *Going Deeper with New Testament Greek*, 193.

David L. Mathewson and Elodie Ballantine Emig cover voice in their intermediate grammar in a separate chapter covering eleven pages.[22] They define voice as the relationship of the grammatical subject to the process expressed in the verb.[23] "The grammatical subject, usually indicated by a nominal form in the nominative case, can be the agent of the action in the verb (i.e., the active voice), the recipient or patient of the action in the verb (i.e., the passive voice), or in some way directly involved in or participating in the action in the verb (i.e., the middle voice)."[24] The voices are to be distinguished from the issue of transitive versus intransitive verbs. There is then a general discussion of the meaning and function of each of the voices, but without the list of copious labels found in other grammars. However, due to some of the difficulties in interpreting and translating the middle voice, the authors do use the labels reflexive, intensive, and reciprocal to describe possible usages. Other topics considered in relation to voice are accusative with passives, expressions of agency with passives, topic continuity, and the effect of the middle on certain verbs (turning transitives into intransitives, changing the meaning of a verb). There is also a brief excursus on deponency, where following recent research the authors question its value and recommend dispensing with it.

Most recently, Heinrich von Siebenthal has produced a reference-type grammar containing much valuable material and treatment of grammatical and syntactical issues. He devotes almost ten pages to the voice system in New Testament Greek and uses slightly more up-to-date language to describe the voices.[25] He begins by defining voice as the subject's relationship to the action expressed by the verb. Voice is to be distinguished from whether verbs are transitive or intransitive; either type of verb can occur with the active, passive, or middle voice. For the specific voices, the active voice presents an action as performed by the subject. In certain verbs it can be used with a force similar to a middle, overlap with the passive, or take a causative sense (determined by the context). The middle voice in Greek indicates greater subject-affectedness. Thus, the middle can be used to

22. Mathewson and Emig, *Intermediate Greek Grammar*, 142–52.
23. Mathewson and Emig, *Intermediate Greek Grammar*, 142.
24. Mathewson and Emig, *Intermediate Greek Grammar*, 142.
25. Von Siebenthal, *Ancient Greek Grammar*, 295–304.

indicate an indirect reflexive, the subject acting on its own body, the subject receiving something, or a direct reflexive middle, reciprocal, or causative. The passive voice is used when the subject is the patient of the action. Passive forms can be used without passive meaning in a causative sense or a "tolerative" (permissive) sense.

What shall we conclude about the previous manner of treating Greek voices in grammars? While voice has certainly received attention by grammarians, and there is some value in the discussion of voice in the above grammars, there are still a number of issues left unresolved by their treatment of voice. First, in much of this work there is little theoretical reflection, even at a basic level, on the semantics of the voice system beyond the general definition of how the subject relates to the action of the verb (perhaps because little specialized work or research has been done on this issue in comparison to verbal aspect; but see below), and there is little consideration of the relationship of the voices to each other in terms of why an author/speaker would select one voice over another and their specific semantics. Second, there is still a tendency to perpetuate a "directional" view of voice, which has to do with the direction of the process away from the subject toward an object (active), toward the subject through an agent (passive), or both away from and back toward the subject (middle).[26] While there is some value in this, much of the treatment of voice in grammars shows little if any development from previous grammatical discussion, and these grammars often appear content to perpetuate previous ways of defining and treating voice. Third, the above approaches follow the common but questionable method of multiplying labels to try to capture the different contexts of usages of the Greek voices and their interpretive and translational significance. Several of the proposed categories of usage seem to depend more on English translation than on the semantics of the voices themselves and lack justification for their usage or criteria for determining how they should be identified and utilized. This also raises the issue of the relationship between these various proposed functions for the voices, since they often do not capture the basic semantic force of the Greek voice (active, passive, or middle). This can be seen by the

---

26. See the visual graphic in Wallace, *Greek Grammar*, 409.

fact that some of the voices apparently have overlapping functions or meanings: reflexive active and reflexive (direct) middle; causative (permissive) active, passive, and middle; passive with middle meaning; deponent middle and passive. This raises the question of the semantics of the voice and the significance of the choice of one voice over another if they can apparently "mean" the same thing in certain contexts. In other words, what is the relationship of the formal endings to the semantics of the three voices?

Fourth, there is still much confusion over the middle voice, with a lack of clear understanding of its semantics beyond general agreement that a reflexive sense is not its primary meaning. It is often merely defined as a middle ground between the active and passive voices, combining the notion of agent and recipient of the action (i.e., a combination of the semantics of the active and passive, with little distinct semantic force of its own), or sometimes only as a sort of "emphatic" active voice. Fifth, the treatment of deponency is ambiguous, with some grammars still finding validity in the concept, while others question its value for interpreting Greek voice, and some fall in between. There is still some misunderstanding on what deponency is ("middle/passive in form but active in meaning"). Finally, with one or two exceptions, insights from modern linguistics have not yet made inroads into grammatical discussion of voice in standard grammars.

Recent Specialized Work on Greek Voice

Outside of this expected and necessary treatment of voice as part of the Greek language in modern-day grammars, work on the Greek voice system has generally lagged behind research and interest in aspect in the Greek verbal system, so that much more work remains to be done on this significant verbal feature. However, recently the employment of the voice system in the New Testament and ancient Greek in general has begun to attract more attention, although the focus has been primarily on the middle voice and deponency, save for one or two exceptions.[27]

27. Harris, "Study of the Greek Language"; Campbell, *Advances in the Study of Greek*, 91–104; Porter, "Did Paul Baptize Himself?"; O'Donnell, "Some New Testament Words"; see more recently O'Donnell's *Corpus Linguistics*, 370–85.

Here I will survey very briefly the most important and relevant work in order to bring the reader of this book up to date on some of the discussion on voice. Again, I will restrict my survey to three of the most recent contributions. The first work summarized below does not focus on New Testament Greek but focuses on ancient Greek more generally and has become somewhat of a standard. The latter two works focus particularly on voice in the Greek of the New Testament—one article length and the other dissertation length.

Rutger Allan

Rutger Allan's work focuses on the meaning of the middle voice in ancient Greek and is one of the first recent comprehensive treatments of voice in Greek.[28] He begins by noting the "puzzling diversity of the different usage types of the middle and passive voice."[29] As a way forward, Allan proposes examining the middle voice in light of prototypical transitive clauses: agent as subject, patient as object, and verb in the active voice. The middle can be seen as a marked departure from this. Allan proposes that what all instances of the middle have in common is the abstract notion of *subject-affectedness*. That is, in comparison with the prototypical transitive clause, the middle is marked coding (a departure from the prototypical transitive clause), where the subject undergoes the effect of the event. Furthermore, Allan understands the middle voice in Greek in terms of both *monosemy* and *polysemy*, as part of a complex network. From a monosemic perspective, the abstract meaning of the middle voice is *subject-affectedness*. However, from a polysemous perspective, the middle voice, while retaining this abstract meaning, takes on various but related meanings: for example, passive use, direct reflexive use, and indirect reflexive use. Thus, "the middle voice is seen as a polysemous network of interrelated meanings. The abstract schema, embodying the semantic commonality of all middle meanings, can be characterized as affectedness of the subject. The different middle meanings can, in turn, be viewed as elaborations of this abstract schema."[30]

28. Allan, *Middle Voice*.
29. Allan, *Middle Voice*, 1.
30. Allan, *Middle Voice*, 57.

Following prototype theory, Allan sees some of these as closer to the prototypical middle meaning, while others are connected to it by extension. Allan then discusses the specific uses of the Greek middle voice under the following eleven categories: (1) passive middle, (2) spontaneous process middle, (3) mental process middle, (4) body motion middle, (5) collective motion middle, (6) reciprocal middle, (7) direct reflexive middle, (8) perception middle, (9) mental activity middle, (10) speech act middle, and (11) indirect reflexive middle.[31] From this listing, it is clear that Allan follows a two-voice system in Greek, seeing the passive (1) as a further function subsumed under the middle. Furthermore, Allan sees the mental process middle (3) as the prototypical middle usage. This also means that the *media tantum*, or middle-only verbs (so-called deponents), fall under the treatment of the middle voice, indicating subject-affectedness. Allan finds no evidence historically that anyone ever "laid aside" active forms (hence deponent), and he notes the diversity of usage of these middle-only verbs. Therefore, these verbs should be treated like other middle verbs that have an active voice opposition, so that categories such as "deponent" are unnecessary to explain verbs that occur only in the middle voice.

Allan also notes the intriguing morphology in the aorist tense with the -(θ)η-, which originally covered passive and spontaneous processes but was extended to cover a number of usages of the middle referenced above (beyond just the passive voice) in Homer and in Classical Greek to include mental process, body motion, and collective motion. The semantic feature that underlies all usages of the aorist passive form is the notion of prototypical patient, whereas for the aorist middle forms the primary feature is the subject as agent. For the -(θ)η- in the future, Allan finds that for many verbs, middle forms are imperfective, and -(θ)η- (passive) forms are aoristic (perfective), so that the distinction between the endings is along the lines of aspect. Finally, he finds a number of examples of verbs where the active and middle overlap in meaning. In these cases, lexically the verb with the active voice semantically indicates subject-affectedness, with the middle voice semantically and redundantly making the subject-affectedness

31. See Allan, *Middle Voice*, chap. 2.

of the verb more salient. The active voice, then, can apparently give way to the subject-affected semantics of the context.

Allan has made an important contribution to the study of the middle voice in the Greek language, though his focus is on Classical Greek. He has effectively demonstrated how the semantic feature of subject-affectedness lies behind all the middle usages. Such an understanding of the middle voice further calls into question the need for such categories as "deponent" to explain verbs that occur only in the middle voice without an active opposition. His work also further supports the notion that Greek began as a two-voice system, with the opposition between active and middle, and with the passive later growing out of the middle. However, Allan's work remains unclear regarding the role that verbal morphology plays in indicating voice. This can be seen in the fact that the middle endings and -(θ)η- endings overlap in their main categories of usage (see above). Furthermore, Allan also appears to suggest that the active voice can be "laid aside" in contexts that indicate subject-affectedness, so that the meaning of the active voice is neutralized in some contexts and with some verbs.[32] This creates ambiguity as to what the voice endings would actually convey, if context can override them. Furthermore, though his focus is on the middle voice, there is little reflection on how the middle forms encode voice within the larger voice system of Greek.

Rachel Aubrey

Rachel Aubrey has produced an important work that focuses mainly on the function of the -(θ)η- ending as it relates to the middle and passive voices in Greek.[33] Much of her work depends on and develops the work of Allan (see above). A concern of grammarians has been what to do with aorist verbs with the "passive" ending -(θ)η- that do not seem to communicate passive semantics in some contexts: the subject is the agent of the verb, as in an active voice. Grammars have resorted to labels such as "passive deponent" or "passive in form but active in meaning" to account for these "exceptions." The concern of Aubrey is to demonstrate that these traditional ways of accounting

---

32. Fletcher, "Voice in the Greek of the New Testament," 99.
33. Aubrey, "Motivated Categories."

for the -(θ)η- ending as exclusively passive, while explaining deviant examples where this ending does not seem to fit passive meaning as a mismatch in form and function, are unnecessary and misguided. Following the theory of cognitive linguistics, the burden of her article is: "Instead of an exclusively passive form with random deviants, -(θ)η- is better understood as a diachronically and synchronically motivated form with multiple functions, all of which fit within the semantic scope of the middle domain."[34] Aubrey resists the notion of limiting -(θ)η- to one morphosyntactical function. Relying on cross-linguistic patterning and prototype theory, she argues that voice is more dynamic with gradual shifts in meaning, rather than distinct categories semantically. She plots event types on a spectrum from more agent-like (active) to more patient-like (passive). The Greek voices (active, middle, passive) are waypoints along this spectrum, not formally restricted and discrete entities. Rather than maintaining strict boundaries, they can blend into each other. She argues that the -(θ)η- ending was originally employed in Greek with the aorist to designate spontaneous events involving a change of state without an external cause (the action is not done by someone or something: e.g., "He died"). However, this allowed it to extend its usage to other more patient-type events, such as the typical passives. According to Aubrey, "middle voice includes both middle and passive semantics within its scope."[35] Like Allan above, she sees the middle voice as indicating subject-affectedness.

Greek sigmatic (-σ-) aorist middle forms, then, were used for more agent-type verbs, and the -(θ)η- for more patient-type verbs, but the latter began to expand into the -σ- territory of more agent-type middle verbs. Therefore, the -(θ)η- ending, which originally was used with patient-like spontaneous actions, extended in two different directions: (1) passive events and (2) middle event types usually expressed with the aorist -σ- endings.[36] According to Aubrey, -(θ)η- aorist verbs are usually used in the New Testament with middle verbs of the patient-type events. In these cases, the -(θ)η- ending "expresses an event in which a single focused participant [the grammatical subject]

34. Aubrey, "Motivated Categories," 565.
35. Aubrey, "Motivated Categories," 586.
36. Aubrey, "Motivated Categories," 573.

undergoes a change of state with no external cause involved in the event."[37] These include spontaneous processes, motion, collective motion, and passives. However, such verbs are also used with middle verbs of more agent-type events. In these cases, the subject of such verbs is both the source and endpoint of the action. Here the more agent-type middle events are direct reflexives/grooming verbs, recip-rocal events, mental activity, speech act, and perception. The aorist ending -(θ)η-, therefore, expands to be used of these event types, hence encroaching on the domain of aorist -σ- verbs.

Aubrey's article has much helpful information and provides a model of how one linguistic method (cognitive linguistics) can shed light on the Greek voice system. However, her work still raises a number of important questions. What are the meanings of the Greek voices, and how are they distinguished? If the -(θ)η- ending can cover such a broad spectrum of event types, and if even the active voice can be considered like the middle voice as subject-affected (where the subject experiences the effects of the action in some way) in in-transitive verbs, there seems to be a frequent mismatch in form and meaning in her paradigm. Her work also raises the question of what role verb morphology plays in indicating voice. Aubrey appears to give more weight to event types and the semantics of the verb than to the morphology of the voice endings. She also raises the question again of whether Koine Greek is a two-voice or three-voice system.

Bryan Fletcher

Bryan Fletcher has recently produced an important study of voice in the Greek of the New Testament and its significance for interpre-tation.[38] Written as a PhD dissertation for McMaster Divinity Col-lege (Hamilton, Ontario), his work is abreast of modern linguistic theory, as well as the history of voice in Proto-Indo European (PIE) languages. His work breaks some new ground on voice by examin-ing the Greek voice system in light of M. A. K. Halliday's Systemic Functional Linguistics. Unlike Allan and Aubrey, he focuses on the entire Greek voice system.

---

37. Aubrey, "Motivated Categories," 595.
38. Fletcher, "Voice in the Greek of the New Testament."

Fletcher defines voice as "the speaker/writer's grammatical portrayal of the role of the subject according to an ergative alignment pattern that is predicated upon causality (startpoint) and affectedness (endpoint) in relation to the verbal process."[39] Fletcher argues that the Greek voice system is an ergative alignment system, which is indicated not by marking nouns in the case endings (as some languages do) but through verbal morphology and the voice system. According to an ergative model, at the center of the clause is the verbal process and a participant that actualizes the process (what he calls the *medium*, following Halliday). In an ergative system, causality (the energy that initiates the process) can be internal or self-generating, or externally initiated by an agent. According to Fletcher, the *agent* is the external cause of the action in a clause, while the *medium* is "the 'conduit' through which the process comes into existence and arrives at actualization. It is the element of the clause that the process finds as its endpoint."[40] Voice, then, concerns the role that the grammatical subject plays in relationship to the verbal process, whether the agent (active) or the medium (middle or passive). These roles are determined not by their case endings but by the verbal voice endings. On this basis, he argues that Greek is a two-voice system, depending primarily on the semantic role of the subject within the ergative aligned voice system. Therefore, the Greek of the New Testament exhibits an active-middle voice opposition. Under the umbrella of the middle voice, the middle can also function as a passive with the addition of the expression of external agency (if expressed with a circumstantial phrase consisting of a prepositional phrase). For Fletcher's model, the primary defining feature of voice is the role of the grammatical subject, whether it functions as the agent (active) or medium (middle, passive) of the verbal process.

According to Fletcher, with the active voice "the subject acts as the original energy source and cause of the verbal process (including intransitive verbs). . . . Causality is the output of energy that resides in the Agent."[41] In the Greek active voice the grammatical subject plays the semantic role of the *agent*. This can potentially affect

39. Fletcher, "Voice in the Greek of the New Testament," 200–201.
40. Fletcher, "Voice in the Greek of the New Testament," 144.
41. Fletcher, "Voice in the Greek of the New Testament," 202.

other participants in the clause, such as a *goal* (grammatical direct object). Fletcher then considers how the active voice functions in certain types of clauses, with other participants, and in participle and infinitive constructions. In light of his definition of verbal voice as an ergative alignment system (see above), Fletcher concludes that "the middle-passive voice portrays the verbal process moving into the subject participant, entering the domain, and being realized in the subject participant as it acts in an endpoint role for the verbal process." Thus, the subject is "the affected participant of the verb, creating a portrayal of the heightened involvement of the subject."[42] That is, the subject is the medium, and thus host to the verbal process.

Throughout Fletcher's discussion, causality is apparently secondary to the role of the subject, and an optional element, in defining the Greek voice system. As with his treatment of the active voice, Fletcher considers the function of the middle in different clause types, with other participants, and in participle and infinitive constructions. The passive voice shares the same subject role as the middle. The subject functions as the medium, the affected participant. However, what distinguishes the function of the passive is the way that causality is conceived. While in the middle voice causality is internal to the process, with the passive voice causality is external to the process; that is, it lies outside the medium + process nucleus. With passives, external causality can be (1) expressed by a circumstantial element (a prepositional phrase; e.g., ὑπό), (2) unspecified and external to the entire clause and inferred from surrounding clauses, or (3) located beyond the wider discourse.[43] Fletcher then examines usages of the passive voice under examples of specified and unspecified agency.

Fletcher, unlike Allan and Aubrey, interprets the -(θ)η- ending as primarily marking passivity in the aorist and future tense forms. In the middle-passive voice, the subject plays the role of medium—that is, the affected participant—though Fletcher is not clear as to why he thinks the middle and passive voices have separate forms in the aorist and future but not in the present and perfect.

42. Fletcher, "Voice in the Greek of the New Testament," 245.
43. Fletcher, "Voice in the Greek of the New Testament," 292.

Fletcher's work provides the most comprehensive and sophisticated examination of the voice system in the Greek of the New Testament to date. He points the way forward to a more robust and linguistically plausible understanding of the voice system, and he further demonstrates the usefulness of SFL as a suitable and adaptable model for understanding features of ancient Greek grammar. He helpfully demonstrates how ergativity can be used in the service of describing the Greek voice system. One issue that his study raises is what role causality plays in the voice system. While it features in his overall definition, he is unclear whether it plays a role in defining the middle voice, though it does at times in his discussion seem to play a role, and a different one from the passive voice. His starting point, rather, is with the role of the subject, whether agent or medium. Furthermore, his study still raises the question of whether Greek is a two-voice or three-voice system.

Conclusion

Some specialized research on the Greek voice system has enhanced our understanding of voice in New Testament Greek. A number of conclusions emerge from the previous survey of research. First, there is still the issue of whether Greek is a two- or three-voice system. Second, there is increasing recognition of the inadequacy of the category of deponency as applied to the middle voice. Third, the above studies raise the need for a clear and robust application of a linguistic model to the voice system of the Greek of the New Testament. Fourth, the emergence of the concept of causality shows promise in explaining the voice system. Finally, there is still a need to demonstrate the relationship of the semantics of the voice system to verbal morphology. These issues pave the way for further work to be done on the Greek voice system.

2

Linguistic Model
and Voice

Linguistic Model

At the outset of this investigation it is important to lay out and summarize the chosen linguistic model from which voice will be examined in this chapter. The studies surveyed in the previous chapter demonstrate the importance of choosing an appropriate linguistic model for this endeavor. In this chapter, I will draw on SFL, especially as developed by M. A. K. Halliday, to analyze the grammatical feature of voice in New Testament Greek (for mood, SFL needs to be significantly adapted).[1] Though I am not claiming that no other linguistic models could be followed, or that this is the only correct model, in this volume SFL proves fruitful in exploring voice in ancient Greek, especially since Halliday gave attention to it. SFL has proven a powerful descriptive model for interpreting the language of the New Testament. It has been successfully adapted for a number of analyses of various features of the Greek language and can be adapted for examining the voice system in the Greek of the New

---

1. See especially Halliday, *Functional Grammar*. Cf. Thompson et al., *Cambridge Handbook*.

Testament.[2] According to Halliday and SFL, language is to be construed as a means of social behavior. It is a way of "doing" things, hence it is functional. The focus of SFL is on how language is used. According to Halliday, language must be seen in terms of how it has been shaped by the functions it has come to serve.[3]

As implied in the name Systemic Functional Linguistics, two primary foci characterize Halliday's functional understanding of language that are important for our discussion of grammatical voice: language as function and language as choice. First, behind Halliday's understanding of grammar is the treatment of language as systemic—that is, a theory of language as choice. "Systemic theory is a theory of meaning as choice, by which a language, or any other semiotic system, is interpreted as a network of interlocking options."[4] The meaning potential of a language thereby emerges from the system of choice generated by its grammar. Thus, SFL places a greater emphasis on *paradigmatic* relationships within grammar. The meaning of each grammatical item is derived from its relationship to other items within the system. That is, "an element is only meaningful if it is defined wholly in terms of other elements. A given linguistic phenomenon that is wholly predetermined, i.e., there is no choice between this and some other grammatical unit, offers little for a discussion of meaning."[5] Therefore, "every expression of meaning through words or grammar implies choice."[6] For example, the different aspects of the Greek verb (imperfective, perfective, stative) should be viewed in relationship to each other, as a system of choices within the verbal network, rather than viewed in isolation as most grammars are prone to do. Consequently, it is significant when an author, for example, chooses to use a present tense form (imperfective aspect) rather than an aorist tense form (perfective aspect) when the author had a choice to use either. When there is no choice to be made (e.g., εἰμί is an aspectually vague verb that offers a choice only in the

2. Cf. Reed, *Discourse Analysis of Philippians*; Martín-Asensio, *Transitivity-Based Foregrounding*; Westfall, *Discourse Analysis*; Peters, *Greek Article*; Porter, *Linguistic Analysis of the Greek New Testament*; Yoon, *Discourse Analysis*.

3. Halliday, *Explorations*; Halliday, *Language as Social Semiotic*.

4. Halliday, *Functional Grammar*, xiv.

5. Porter, *Verbal Aspect*, 12.

6. Tan, "Prominence in the Pauline Letters," 97.

imperfective aspect, with no aorist forms),[7] no interpretive significance can be attached to the verb form.

Second, SFL considers how language is used to do things. According to Halliday, the function of language is constrained by its context of situation: the field, tenor, and mode of discourse. Language has three metafunctions: ideational, interpersonal, and textual. The *ideational function* refers to the ability of language to represent our experiences, often what we think of as the "content" of a discourse. The *interpersonal function* of language concerns "the speaker or writer doing something to the listener or reader by means of language."[8] This is the use of language to express social and personal relationships.[9] The *textual function* of language focuses on the function of language to construct a message and considers such things as theme and prominence. All three metafunctions are found in a clause; that is, a clause can be analyzed from the perspective of its interpersonal, ideational, and textual metafunctions. However, it is Halliday's ideational metafunction, which concerns the transitivity system in language (the relationship of participants to the action), that is the most relevant to our discussion of voice in Greek (for the interpersonal metafunction, see below on mood).

Transitivity and Ergativity

Halliday addresses voice as part of his discussion on transitivity within the ideational or experiential metafunction of language.[10] Porter states that certain features—such as "subject matter, semantic domains, and participants—constitute the basic semantic material of the ideational metafunction. What the author is saying about these semantic components is expressed through the transitivity network."[11]

7. The verb εἰμί also exhibits future tense forms, but the future tense form is best treated as not fully aspectual and is in some ways more closely related to the mood system. See Porter, *Verbal Aspect*, 403–39.

8. Halliday, *Functional Grammar*, 53.

9. Halliday, *Explorations*, 41.

10. Halliday, *Functional Grammar*, 144–54.

11. Porter, *Linguistic Analysis of the Greek New Testament*, 152. The entirety of chap. 9, "The Ideational Metafunction and Register," presents a competent example

The ideational function of language is basically "what the discourse is about." At the heart of the ideational metafunction of language is the transitivity system. The transitivity system in language, according to Halliday, "specifies the different types of processes that are recognized in the language, and the structures by which they are expressed."[12] As such, a process consists of three semantic features: (1) the *process* itself, (2) the *participants* in the process, and (3) the *circumstances* associated with the process.[13] These three function at the level of the clause and make up the system of transitivity, according to Halliday. Thus, a full transitivity analysis, belonging to the ideational function of language, takes into consideration all three, which refer to the "goings on" in a text.

The participants in a text include the *actor* (usually the grammatical subject) and the *goal* (usually the grammatical object) of the clause affected by the verbal process. The participants play different roles in relationship to and determined by the process types (see below). The process, then, is the verbal process indicated by the predicate, or verb form. The processes can be divided, according to Halliday, into further process types: for example, material, mental, or relational. The circumstances of a clause are indicated by prepositional phrases, adverbs, or other structures and indicate notions such as time, location, manner, and so on. A full consideration of the transitivity structure of a clause analyzes all three of these features, or in simpler terms, transitivity analyzes "who does what to whom."[14]

It is as part of the transitivity system that Halliday discusses voice, since voice is concerned with the relationship between a process and its participants. However, an analysis of voice is a further stage in the analysis of transitivity in that it asks the question of causality: How is the process brought about in relationship to the participant engaged in it? While in a transitivity-based analysis clauses are categorized according to process types and the differing roles the participants

---

of the potential for application of SFL's ideational metafunction of language to the analysis of the Greek NT.

12. Halliday, *Functional Grammar*, 101. As will be discussed below, according to Halliday, the transitivity network in a language is part of the ideational metafunction of the clause.

13. Halliday, *Functional Grammar*, 101.

14. Cf. Martín-Asensio, *Transitivity-Based Foregrounding*, 12–13.

perform in relation to the *kinds of processes*, voice deals with the clause in terms of how the participant relates to the verbal process regarding *causality and agency*. Ultimately, an analysis of transitivity, therefore, also considers voice, causality, and agency in relationship to the participants. This means that transitivity in its narrow sense (that is, whether an action extends beyond the subject to an object) and in the broader sense in Halliday's discussion above are both to be distinguished from, but at the same time also related to, voice by addressing the features of causality and agency within the discussions of transitivity (see below).

It is in his treatment of transitivity that Halliday introduces a further concept that is important for our understanding of voice: *ergativity*.[15] As noted above, the transitivity system consists of processes, participants, and circumstances in the clause. Transitivity analysis considers the types of processes and the roles of the participants in relation to the process. Within the transitivity system, *voice* considers the relationship between those participants and the process (verbal clause) in terms of agency and causality. A fruitful way to analyze this relationship is through analyzing the clause in terms of ergativity. In Halliday's ergativity-based analysis, the main issue is whether the participant engaged in a process brings about the action, or whether the action is brought about by another entity.[16] "Either the process is represented as self-engendering, in which case there is no separate Agent; or it is represented as engendered from outside, in which case there is another participant functioning as Agent."[17] More concisely, "Is the process brought about from within, or from outside?"[18] That is, in an ergativity-based interpretation of a clause, the notions of causality and agency play focal roles. According to Halliday, if the action is self-engendered, with no reference to an outside cause, the clause is nonergative. If the process has an external cause in its clause, and it is brought about by an agent, then the clause is ergative. At this point Halliday introduces another important term:

15. See Halliday, *Functional Grammar*, 144–54; Halliday and Matthiessen, *Functional Grammar*, 280–301; Thompson, *Introducing Functional Grammar*, 135–38.
16. Halliday, *Functional Grammar*, 145.
17. Halliday and Matthiessen, *Functional Grammar*, 290.
18. Halliday and Matthiessen, *Functional Grammar*, 290.

medium. The medium is "the entity through the medium of which the process comes into existence."[19] It is the thing through which the process is actualized. It will be the direct object in a transitive clause (He opened the *door*), but it is also the subject in an intransitive clause (The *door* opened). The other important participant is what Halliday calls the *agent*, which functions as the external cause of the action. It will be the subject in a transitive clause (*He* opened the door) or in a prepositional phrase in an intransitive clause (The door was opened *by him*). *Medium* and *agent* are functional terms that relate to causality and agency. In summary, in transitive clauses (which take a direct object) the agent will be the subject, and the medium will be the object; in intransitive clauses (which do not take a direct object), the medium will be the subject.

Ergativity has become a much-discussed term in linguistics. In languages that express ergativity, according to R. M. W. Dixon, "the intransitive subject is treated in the same manner as transitive object, and differently from transitive subject."[20] That is, the subject of the *intransitive* verb functions in the same way as the object of the *transitive* verb. But the subject of the *transitive* verb functions differently. "The subject of an intransitive verb 'becomes' the object of a corresponding transitive verb, and a new *ergative* subject is introduced as the 'agent' (or 'cause') of the action referred to."[21] Consider the following sentences:

Mary sailed the boat.
The boat sailed.

In the two sentences, the term "boat," according to Halliday's analysis, functions as the medium in both of these instances, even though "boat" is the direct object in the first sentence and the subject in the second. That is, "boat" is the medium through which the process of the verb ("sail") takes place or the entity that is affected by the action in both examples above. Furthermore, the subjects of both sentences, "Mary" and "boat," do not function in the same way,

19. Halliday and Matthiessen, *Functional Grammar*, 146.
20. Dixon, "Ergativity," 60–61.
21. Lyons, *Theoretical Linguistics*, 352.

though both are grammatically the subject of the clause. In the first example, "Mary" is the subject and the agent, or the external cause of the action of sailing. The object "boat" is the medium, the thing through which the process (sailing) is actualized. However, in the second clause the subject "boat" is not the agent but still the medium; that is, it functions in the same way as the direct object "boat" in the first clause. In this second sentence there is no specific reference to an agent. The action, then, is seen as self-engendering, occurring from within, with no reference to an external cause. Hence it is ergative.[22] It is important to recognize that Halliday's understanding of ergativity and internally and externally caused action is limited to the contrast between transitive and intransitive pairs in the English language. In certain types of processes (often causative), the object of a transitive verb can become the subject of a corresponding intransitive verb (Halliday labels both of these as the *medium*). Thus, the direct object "boat" in the first, transitive clause above functions in the same way as the subject "boat" in the second, intransitive clause above. In the sentence "She increased her profits," the clause is transitive and contains an object ("profits") of the verb "increased." However, the object can become the subject of the same verb used intransitively: "Her profits increased." In both cases "profits" is the medium through which the action is actualized. The former contains a direct agent or cause ("she"), while the latter is internal or self-caused with no explicit agent. Halliday's treatment of ergativity is restricted to verbs of this type. As will be seen below, ergativity in Greek depends not on the transitive/intransitive contrast but on the verbal endings that indicate voice.

How this translates into voice, according to Halliday, is that a clause that lacks an expression of direct agency (the action is internally caused) is middle. A clause expressing agency (nonmiddle) is either active, where the subject is the agent, or passive, where the subject is the medium and the agent is expressed, if at all, by some other means (a circumstantial element such as a prepositional phrase: The boat was sailed *by Mary*). These insights on ergativity

22. However, there is a discernable difference in Halliday's terminology. He understands verbs that take an agent, the active or passive, as *ergative*, whereas verbs that express no agent (middle) are *nonergative* (*Functional Grammar*, 145–47).

and voice from Halliday and SFL have potential for understanding the Greek voice system. However, at least two factors caution against a blanket application of Halliday's approach to voice in the Greek of the New Testament. First, Halliday's approach was developed for the English language. As seen above, ergativity in the English language is limited to certain verbs (often causal) whose objects in a transitive clause (Mary sailed the *boat*) function in the same way as the subjects in a corresponding intransitive clause (The *boat* sailed). Yet ergativity in Greek is not limited to the transitive/intransitive pairing but is encoded morphologically in the middle voice form. The Greek middle voice can be used with transitive or intransitive verbs. The role of the subject as agent or medium in Greek does not depend on whether it occurs in a transitive or intransitive clause but depends on the voice of the verb. Second, English has no middle voice like Greek, though middle meaning could be communicated in English lexically.

The Meaning of Voice and the Greek Voice System

According to Bryan Fletcher, "Greek belonged to the Indo-European family of languages," and the ancient Greeks understood voice as conveying "a semantic condition, state, or disposition of the verb that is conferred onto the grammatical subject in relation to the verbal process."[23] Thus, voice is usually defined as primarily concerning the relationship of the grammatical subject (usually expressed by a nominal in the nominative case) to the action indicated by the verb. The nuclear unit for voice is the subject and verb (S + V). Therefore, verbal voice is part of the transitivity system of language in that it considers how the subject relates to the verbal process. According to Mathewson and Emig, "Voice indicates the role the subject of a clause plays with respect to the verb's action."[24] Or, as von Siebenthal says, "Voice is about the *relation between the subject and the 'action'* expressed by the verb, indicating in what ways the subject entity is

23. Fletcher, "Voice in the Greek of the New Testament," 43.
24. Mathewson and Emig, *Intermediate Greek Grammar*, 142. See also Porter, *Idioms*, 50.

meant to be involved in the action."[25] Thus, the subject can be seen as directly bringing about the action, as the recipient of the action, or as being involved in the action in some way.

However, as mentioned above, more recently in light of SFL's treatment of voice and ergativity, Porter and others have begun to develop the view that voice is a category that also indicates *causality*, whether an action is directly caused, externally/indirectly caused, or internally caused (ergative). "Causality in a clause involves the output of energy that brings the process about."[26] Thus, Matthew Brook O'Donnell defines voice as "a semantic category by which a speaker/writer grammaticalizes a perspective on how a process is caused through the selection of a particular voice form."[27] More specifically, voice in Greek indicates a perspective on how a process is caused in relationship to the role of the subject within the verbal complex. Greek voice indicates where causality and agency lie in relationship to the S + V complex.

Porter aptly captures both features—the relationship of the gram-matical *subject* to the action, and the feature of *causality*—in his definition of voice for Greek verbs: "The Greek voice-form system grammaticalizes the causality system in Greek, that is, the semantic relationship between actions and their causes, and whether and how these causes are linked to the subjects as agents and patients in these processes."[28] More recently, and also combining both causality and the relationship of the grammatical subject, though focusing more on the role of the grammatical subject, Fletcher has defined voice as "the speaker/writer's grammatical portrayal of the role of the subject according to an ergative alignment pattern that is predicated upon causality (startpoint) and affectedness (endpoint) in relation to the verbal process."[29] Therefore, voice can be seen to indicate causality and how the grammatical subject (expressed or implied) of a clause is

---

25. Von Siebenthal, *Ancient Greek Grammar*, 295. Emphasis is his. Cf. also Wallace, *Greek Grammar*, 408.

26. Fletcher, "Voice in the Greek of the New Testament," 137.

27. O'Donnell, *Corpus Linguistics*, 371.

28. Porter, "Did Paul Baptize Himself?," 109. This is something of an advance over his definition that follows a standard way of defining Greek voice, which focuses on the grammatical subject, in his earlier work in *Idioms*, 50.

29. Fletcher, "Voice in the Greek of the New Testament," 245.

connected to the cause of an action, whether as the agent or medium. In other words, it seems to me that causality is the main semantic feature indicated by the selection of a given voice form and that accounts for its various usages in the Greek of the New Testament. Then the selection of the voice form in terms of causality affects the function of the subject in relationship to causality, whether it is the agent (the initiator of the action) or the medium (the affected participant). The active voice indicates direct causality and agency of the subject. The middle voice indicates internal causality and subject-affectedness but lacks any external agency. The passive indicates external/indirect causality with subject-affectedness. As seen above, voice is related to ergativity, which in Greek is expressed by the verbal endings. Unlike languages such as English, ergative voice, then, is not restricted by verbs that are transitive or intransitive, but by choice among the Greek voices of the middle voice form.[30] Also, the role of the subject as *agent* or *medium* is not indicated morphologically (the subject is normally nominative) or through a transitive construction but is determined by the active or middle/passive voices.

Porter in a preliminary way has developed the definition of the Greek voice system in terms of causality.[31] The active voice indicates direct causality (subject as agent or direct cause) while the passive voice indicates indirect causality (subject as recipient with a separate external agent); that is, the participant that functions as agent has an indirect relationship to the process from outside the S + V complex, being embedded in a circumstantial (prepositional) phrase. The middle (ergative) voice indicates internal causality; that is, the action is *not* brought about by an external cause or agent, but its cause is

30. On ergativity, see Dixon, "Ergativity"; *Collins COBUILD*, 155–57. On application of ergativity to Greek voice, see Fletcher, "Voice in the Greek of the New Testament." The *Collins COBUILD English Grammar* defines ergative verbs in this way: "Verbs which can have the same things as their object, when transitive, or their subject, when intransitive, are called *ergative verbs*" (156, emphasis is theirs). The *Collins COBUILD English grammar* provides a list of verbs in English that can be considered ergative on pp. 156–57—for example, verbs that describe a change (e.g., begin, break, dry), or verbs that describe physical movement (e.g., spin, shake, stand). Again, Greek does not indicate ergativity by distinguishing the object and subject of ergative verbs based on case endings, or based on the transitive versus intransitive distinction, but uses verb endings that indicate voice.

31. See also Porter, "Did Paul Baptize Himself?"; Porter, "Prominence," 64–65.

internal to the process or engendered within the process itself, with an emphasis on the involvement of the subject in the action. Fletcher says that the subject in middle verbs is marked for affectedness.[32] Consequently, O'Donnell suggests the following tentative definitions for the three Greek voices based upon the semantic feature of causality:

> *Direct causality* is the meaning of the active voice form: the cause of the process is attributed to the actor of the process (grammatical subject for finite forms or logical subject for nonfinite forms) of the verbal form.
>
> *External causality* is the meaning of the passive voice form: the cause of the process is attributed to some external entity, which may or may not be grammaticalized in the immediate clause structure or the surrounding co-text.
>
> *Internal causality* is the meaning of the middle voice form: the cause of the process is attributed to elements within the process itself, in which the actor is involved.[33]

To summarize, the Greek voice system should be defined in terms of causality. But the relationship of the subject to the verbal process should be defined in terms of how that relates to causality and agency. In these terms, the active voice expresses direct causality, and the subject functions as the explicit agent or initiator of the action. With the passive voice, cause is external to the process, and the subject is not the agent but the medium and affected entity of the process. The cause of the action is expressed indirectly by an external agent explicitly (by an adjunct prepositional phrase) or implicitly (by broader contextual features). The passive and middle voices are related in that the subject does not directly cause the action but is affected by or involved in the action in some way in both instances— that is, it is the medium. What distinguishes the two voices is the different perspective on causality and agency. With the passive voice there is an external agent and cause, expressed by a circumstantial

---

32. Fletcher, "Voice in the Greek of the New Testament," 245–50.

33. O'Donnell, *Corpus Linguistics*, 371. He has also intentionally modeled this threefold depiction on the threefold view of aspect in Porter, *Verbal Aspect*; Porter, *Idioms*.

element (a prepositional phrase), if specified. However, with the middle voice there is no external agency, and the action is internally caused (ergative).[34] Or, with the middle voice the cause of the action originates within the medium + process complex, and agency is implicit with the medium and process, whereas with the passive voice the cause of the action originates outside of and external to the medium + process configuration.

To describe the voices in a slightly different way, with the *active voice*, agency and causality arise solely with the grammatical subject in the S + V complex (direct agency). With the *passive voice*, agency arises outside of the S + V complex in the form of a modifying prepositional phrase, if expressed (indirect/external agency). With the *middle voice*, causality arises within the S + V complex, with the subject being in some way involved in and affected by the action (internal causality). On the basis of causality, Greek could be considered a three-voice system, with three different means of expressing causality.

Finally, the role of the subject as agent or medium is demonstrated not by the case endings of nouns (subjects are generally always nominative in Greek) but by the verbal endings—active, passive, and middle voice forms.[35] As seen above, the role of the subject as agent or medium is not the entry point for voice but the effect of choosing a perspective on causality. Therefore, based on the above discussion, the following chart compares the three voices in Greek in relationship to the functional role of the grammatical subject and to causality and agency.

Voice	Relation to causality/agency	Functional role of subject
Active	Direct	Agent
Passive	Indirect—external	Medium (affected)
Middle	Indirect—internal	Medium (affected)

34. A similar perspective is summarized in Porter, "Did Paul Baptize Himself?," 108; O'Donnell, *Corpus Linguistics*, 370–86.

35. As Fletcher concludes, "The subject participant roles of Agent and Medium and what these mean in function, are always encoded by their respective voice forms" ("Voice in the Greek of the New Testament," 197).

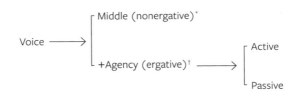

Figure 2.1

---

* Halliday, *Functional Grammar*, 146.
† Halliday, *Functional Grammar*, 147.

We can therefore conclude that Greek voice indicates how the grammatical subject relates to the verbal process in relation to causality and agency. The three Greek voices will be discussed in greater detail below.

The above discussion of voice in Greek suggests that each voice should be understood in relationship to the others as an overall network of choices. One possible way of conceiving of the voice system, following Halliday's treatment of voice and ergativity, would be in terms of the choice between external causality (Halliday's ergative) and internal causality (Halliday's nonergative).[36]

The entry condition of voice confronts the speaker/writer with the choice between +agency and middle (see fig. 2.1). The choice of +agency would then require a further choice between direct causality (active voice) and indirect causality (passive voice). The choice of middle or internal (self-engendered) causality would require the choice of the middle voice. In this case, the active and passive forms are related through the feature of +agency. They are distinguished in terms of where agency lies—in the subject (active) or in an adjunct/prepositional phrase (passive). The problem with this system display, at least for Greek, is that it does not account for the middle voice (internal causality) as the most marked voice (demonstrated by its distributional infrequency) and the most delicate (specific and meaningful) choice semantically from the system. It also misses the relationship between the middle and passive voices, where the subject

36. See Halliday, *Functional Grammar*, 151.

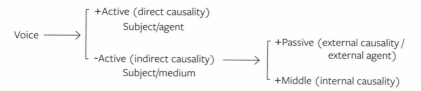

Figure 2.2

This is a slight modification of Porter and O'Donnell, "Greek Verbal System," 17. See also O'Donnell, *Corpus Linguistics*, 372. For an application of a network display to verbal aspect, see Porter, *Verbal Aspect*, 90–109.

is functioning not as the agent but as medium, under Halliday's own approach. Most scholars agree that there is a relationship between the middle and passive voice diachronically. Furthermore, Halliday's ergativity should be used to refer to internally caused actions (middle) rather than to externally caused actions (active and passive). The latter indicates nonergativity.

Therefore, a better way of displaying the network of choices in the Greek voice system and the relationship of the voices to each other is illustrated in figure 2.2.

Within the verbal voice system, with the entry condition of "voice" a speaker/writer must choose between the features of +active or -active. The starting point for the voice system is causality. The +active indicates direct causality and is realized by the active voice form, which is the least heavily weighted voice form. The grammatical subject then functions as the direct agent. The choice of -active indicates indirect causality, where the subject functions as medium, which requires a further choice between +passive and +middle, realized with the passive voice and middle voice forms, respectively. In this case, the middle and passive voices are related in that the subject is not the agent of the process, but the medium, affected participant, and causality are indirect. The passive and middle voice are distinguished, though, through their perspective on causality and agency, the passive indicating external causality and the middle, internal causality or ergativity. Thus, this display helpfully conceives of the choices as a series of increasingly specific selections in terms of causality, from direct to indirect, external to internal causality, and the differing roles of the subject, with the middle voice being distributionally the most significant choice semantically. It also recognizes the connection between the passive and middle voice in terms of the subject not being the agent (indirect causality) but being involved in the action in some way as the medium (to use Halliday's terms).

Like verbal aspect, voice indicates a *perspective* on the action from the standpoint of causality and the relationship of the subject to causality, indicated by the author's choice of a given morphological ending. It is largely "a subjective decision on the part of the writer or speaker."[37] According to Albert Rijksbaron, "Voice, then, enables the language user to vary the *perspective* from which persons and other entities involved in a given state of affairs are presented."[38] More specifically, it indicates "a *perspective* on how a process is caused."[39] Thus, consider the following Greek sentences:

εἴτε γλῶσσαι, παύσονται. (1 Cor. 13:8)

Whether tongues, *they will cease.*

οὐδεὶς ἄξιος εὑρέθη ἀνοῖξαι τὸ βιβλίον οὔτε βλέπειν αὐτό. (Rev. 5:4)

No one *was found* worthy to open the scroll or to look at it.

In the first sentence, which contains a middle voice form (παύσονται), an agent could in fact be present in reality (an external cause to the cessation of tongues), but the choice of the middle voice παύσονται indicates the author's desire not to mention an external agent and to present and foreground both the action as internally caused and its effect on the subject (see "Intransitive Clauses" under the discussion of the middle voice in chap. 3).[40] In the second sentence, the verb is in the passive voice (εὑρέθη), indicating external causality and that the subject οὐδεὶς is the medium or recipient of the action. In this

---

37. Young, *Intermediate New Testament Greek*, 133.

38. Rijksbaron, *Syntax and Semantics*, 134. Italics his.

39. O'Donnell, *Corpus Linguistics*, 371. Italics mine. Cf. Fletcher, "Voice in the Greek of the New Testament," 245.

40. For detailed treatment of the middle voice in this text, see Porter, *Idioms*, 69; Carson, *Exegetical Fallacies*, 75–77. Cf. Wallace, *Greek Grammar*, 422–23.

clause the agent of the action is left unexpressed.[41] The author could have used an active voice form to focus on the agent of the action of finding (X found no one worthy). But by using the passive form, the author focuses attention on the subject (οὐδεὶς), the lack of anyone worthy who could be found, rather than on the agent of the process of finding. In this way, by the selection of a given voice, an author provides a certain perspective on or portrayal of the relationship of the grammatical subject to the process in terms of causality and affectedness.

Verbal voice, like verbal aspect, is a formally based semantic category, or as Porter puts it, "Voice is a form-based semantic category used to describe the role that the grammatical subject plays in relation to an action."[42] As such, voice in Greek is grammaticalized in all the moods (indicative, subjunctive, optative, imperative) and verbal forms (finite and nonfinite [infinitives and participles]). As already seen, and as will be argued further below, there are three voices in the Greek voice system: active, passive, middle. Regarding morphology, most verbs in all aspects (perfective, imperfective, stative; see also the future) have a distinct set of formal endings for indicating the active voice. However, in the imperfective (present/imperfect) and stative tenses/aspects (perfect/pluperfect) one set of forms does "double duty" for both the passive and middle voices, while with the aorist and future tense forms there are separate middle and passive forms.

	Middle	Passive
Present/Imperfect	-ομαι/-ομην	(-ομαι/-ομην)
Stative	-μαι	(-μαι)

| 1st Aorist/2nd Aorist | -σαμην/-ομην | -(θ)η- |
| Future | -σομαι | -θήσομαι |

41. The lack of expressed agency in Rev. 5:4 also creates ambiguity in this context as to the agent's identity. That is, it is not clear in the context whether it is John or the angel (or someone else in heaven) who searched for one worthy to open the scroll. John is pictured as weeping in the immediately previous clause, but it is still not clear whether he was the one who was not able to find anyone worthy to open the scroll. Perhaps the ambiguity with the passive voice is intentional.

42. Porter, *Idioms*, 62.

Since the middle and passive voices cannot be distinguished morphologically in the imperfective and stative aspects, interpreters usually point to contextual features for distinguishing the two voices[43]—for example, the presence of an agent expressed in the form of a prepositional phrase (e.g., ὑπό and a noun in the genitive case; ἐν and a noun in the dative case).

καὶ ἦν ἐν τῇ ἐρήμῳ τεσσεράκοντα ἡμέρας πειραζόμενος <u>ὑπὸ τοῦ σατανᾶ</u>. (Mark 1:13)

And he was in the wilderness for forty days *being tempted* <u>by Satan</u>.

> The implied subject of "being tempted" is Jesus, and the agent is expressed by the prepositional phrase (ὑπὸ τοῦ σατανᾶ), showing πειραζόμενος to be passive.

Then, there are a number of verbs that do not take active forms but use only middle/passive forms, the so-called deponent verbs (see below on deponency). That is, within their paradigm they offer no choice formally in the active voice. Again, several of these verbs that take only middle/passive endings have only one set of endings.

	Active	Middle
ἔρχομαι	——	ἔρχομαι
δέχομαι	——	δέχομαι

However, some other verbs that also exhibit no active forms take separate middle endings for the imperfective, perfective, and/or stative, as well as a separate set of passive -(θ)η- endings for the perfective aspect in their paradigm.

	Active	Middle	Passive
ἀποκρίνομαι	—	ἀποκρίνομαι / ἀπεκρινάμην	ἀπεκρίθην
γίνομαι	—	γίνομαι / ἐγένομην	ἐγενήθην

---

43. Van Emde Boas et al., *Cambridge Grammar of Classical Greek*, 448, 450.

In addition, some verbs, while exhibiting active endings in the present tense, take only middle/passive endings for a different tense form (e.g., future).

	Present	Future
γινώσκω	γινώσκω	γνώσομαι

The above discussion represents some of the formal considerations that will provide the basis for the following further discussion of voice in the Greek of the New Testament.

Relationship of Voice to Transitivity

In discussing the Greek voice system, it is necessary and helpful to distinguish voice from the related but distinct concept of transitivity. Greek grammars usually point out that voice is not the same thing as transitivity.[44] As A. T. Robertson has observed, "Voice *per se* does not deal with the question of transitive or intransitive action."[45] The notion of transitivity is used in two slightly different ways in modern grammatical discussion. In traditional grammatical description, transitivity is usually understood in a limited way to refer to whether a verb in a clause takes an object or not.[46] Verbs that take an object—that is, they extend themselves to a recipient (or goal) of the action—are considered transitive. However, verbs that do not so extend themselves—that is, they include only one participant (the grammatical subject, or agent) and do not take a direct object—are considered intransitive. Linguists sometimes refer to these as "one-place" and "two-place verbs." Verbs that are "one-place" (intransitive) require only one nominal, a subject (*She* ran), whereas "two-place" verbs (transitive) take two nominals, one the subject and the other the object (*He* hit *the ball*).[47] The main question is whether the action extends itself beyond the

---

44. Wallace, *Greek Grammar*, 409.
45. Robertson, *Grammar of the Greek New Testament*, 797.
46. Wallace, *Greek Grammar*, 409.
47. See Lyons, *Theoretical Linguistics*, 350.

actor (the grammatical subject) to another entity (the direct object) or not.[48]

The student studied.

> Intransitive; the action does not extend itself to another participant, an object.

The student studied *Greek*.

> Transitive; the action extends itself to another participant, an object.

Ἐὰν οὖν *προσφέρῃς* τὸ δῶρόν σου ἐπὶ τὸ θυσιαστήριον (Matt. 5:23)
If, therefore, you *offer* your gift upon the altar

> The verb is transitive; the action extends itself to another participant, the object τὸ δῶρόν.

πάντες γὰρ *ἥμαρτον*. (Rom. 3:23)
For all *have sinned*.

> The verb is intransitive; the action does not extend itself to another participant, an object.

As already noted above, the concept of transitivity is utilized in a very different, broader, and more complex manner in SFL where it refers to the entire clause, not just the verb and the object (or lack of). This concept considers the process types, the role of the participants according to the process type, and the circumstances. The following sentence will be used to illustrate an analysis of the clause in terms of SFL's transitivity system.

ὅτι *εἶδον* οἱ ὀφθαλμοί μου τὸ σωτήριόν σου. (Luke 2:30)
For my eyes *have seen* your salvation.

---

48. Halliday and Matthiessen, *Functional Grammar*, 287. Zúñiga and Kittilä describe it in terms of monovalent or bivalent (*Grammatical Voice*, 3–4).

In this clause, the two participants are "eyes" and "salvation." The verbal process "have seen" is a mental-process-type verb that can be further described as a verb of perception.[49] The subject of the clause, "eyes," is the sensor of the verb of mental process, and the object, "salvation," is the phenomenon, or what is sensed or perceived.

Obviously, there is some overlap with both of the above notions of transitivity and grammatical voice, in that both concern the relationship between the process and its participants. Voice, as it relates to causality within the clause, can be seen as a feature within the transitivity system. In that a transitivity analysis considers the process and participants of a clause and their semantic roles and relationships, the analysis of voice is a further stage that considers what brought about, or caused, the process within the analysis of transitivity and how this relates to the grammatical subject participant. In this sense, transitivity and voice are different perspectives on the process and participants. In the traditional understanding, transitive versus intransitive has to do with *extension* (whether a verbal process is extended to an object or goal), whereas voice has to do with *causation* (how the verbal process is brought about).[50] Transitivity analyzes the process and the role of the participants, whereas voice analyzes the relationship between the participants and the process in terms of agency and causality. The following sentence will serve to illustrate the two types of analysis: transitivity and voice or causality.

Καὶ εὐθὺς τὸ πνεῦμα αὐτὸν ἐκβάλλει εἰς τὴν ἔρημον. (Mark 1:12)
And immediately the Spirit cast him out into the wilderness.

In this sentence, under a transitivity-type analysis, "Spirit" and "him" are both participants, with "Spirit" being the actor in relationship to the activity-type process of casting out and the participant, "him," functioning as the goal. One could also say that the verb ("cast out") is transitive, since it extends its action to another participant, a direct object in the accusative case ("him"). However, according to analysis

---

49. For this process type and the role of the participants, see Halliday, *Functional Grammar*, 106–12.

50. Halliday, *Functional Grammar*, 145.

along the lines of voice and causality, "Spirit" is the agent that directly causes (active voice) or brings about the process of casting out, with the pronoun "him" being the entity affected by the action, or the medium through which the action takes place. Understood in this way, voice, causality, and agency can be seen as important parts of the transitivity system in language.

The Number of Voices in the Greek of the New Testament

As noted above, some verb tenses (aspects) have only one set of endings, which grammatically have a "dual function" to specify both the middle and passive voices (present, imperfect, perfect). However, other verb tenses apparently exhibit separate endings for the middle and passive voices (aorist, future). This raises the question of the exact number of voices in Greek, whether it is a dual-voice system or tri-voice system. It also raises the issue of the relationship between the voices synchronically and in light of their diachronic development. "The history and development of the three voices of Greek—active, middle and passive—are complex and uncertain."[51] There is general agreement, despite the manner in which voice is treated in most grammars, that the Greek language developed as an active-middle voice system, and that the passive was a later development from the middle voice. This is not the place to explore diachronically the history of voice, but we will simply note the relationship of the middle and passive voices in the Greek language. Allan and Aubrey (see above) argue for a two-voice system. Fletcher more recently has also argued for a two-voice system based on the similar function of the subject as medium with both the middle and passive voices. He sees the passive as simply another function of the middle voice.

While it makes good sense to see the passive voice as a further extension of the middle, or a further function, there are also reasons to consider it as a third, distinct voice. First, despite the fact that the middle and passive have identical endings in the present and

51. Porter, *Idioms*, 62.

perfect, for the aorist and future two distinct sets of endings did develop, the -σ- and -(θ)η- for the middle and passive, respectively (see below). "In the NT, the theta form becomes exclusively passive in its use when a verb has two middle-passive forms that are in use: a theta form in addition to a -μην or -μαι form to express middle passive voice."[52] Therefore, it is possible that for the aorist and future, which are similar morphologically, the -(θ)η- was used to distinguish the third voice (passive), whereas the present and perfect forms, the more marked forms, experienced formal syncretization and distinguished the middle and passive on a contextual basis.[53] However, it is possible that the -(θ)η- for some verbs also extended its meaning to cover some middle meanings.[54] Second, a stronger basis for distinguishing the three voices semantically is the different perspectives on causality that each of the voices conveys. As seen above, the active voice indicates direct causality, with the subject functioning as agent. It is true that the middle and passive voices exhibit a similar function for the grammatical subject, the medium or affected participant. However, if causality is part of the semantics (or, I would argue, the main focus) of the voice system, then the two voices can be distinguished based on their level of causality. The middle indicates internal causality that arises from the medium + process complex. Even if one were to argue that the passive was subsumed under the middle voice, the passive voice still manifests a different perspective on causality: while the subject functions as the affected element as with the middle, the passive voice signals external causality, where cause is external to the medium and process, being located in a circumstantial expression (prepositional phrase) or implied in the broader context. In this way, most modern-day grammars are correct in distinguishing three separate voices, with different perspectives on the way in which the action comes about and the role the grammatical subject plays. So at the very least, it is possible to distinguish two separate functions of the middle voice based on morphology in the aorist and future, and based on different perspectives on causality (external and internal).

52. Fletcher, "Voice in the Greek of the New Testament," 314.
53. Stanley E. Porter, in private correspondence, May 5, 2020.
54. See Aubrey, "Motivated Categories."

The Role of -(θ)η-

Closely related to the previous discussion is the function of the -(θ)η- ending for the aorist and future verbal forms.[55] As already noted above, in the work of Allan and Aubrey, two of the more extensive treatments of voice in ancient Greek, the -(θ)η- formal ending is understood as a polysemous ending, which performs a sort of "double duty," covering both middle and passive meanings in the Greek voice system. Aubrey has argued that -(θ)η- originated as a middle marker of spontaneous event types and later expanded to include more patient-like events (hence, passives).[56] However, Fletcher has argued that in verbs that take a separate -(θ)η- form along with -μην or -μαι forms, "the -μην forms express middle use and the theta forms express passive use, having either specified or unspecified agency."[57] "The theta form exists in addition to the other forms used to express middle-passive voice in the aorist and future tense-forms, giving these tense-forms two forms for the middle-passive voice."[58]

Therefore, whatever their precise origins, it appears that two separate forms grew up around the middle and passive voice that create a division of labor, since Greek normally does not tolerate formal redundancy. While there may be some instances of -(θ)η- taking on middle meaning, as Allan and Aubrey propose, in most instances the -(θ)η- can be understood as indicating passive meaning, especially with verbs that take both -μην or -μαι forms and -(θ)η-. The -μην or -μαι forms will communicate middle meaning. Therefore, the aorist and future have distinct forms in the middle-passive voice, so that all three voices are inflected.[59]

	Active	Middle	Passive
1st Aorist	-σα	-σαμην	-(θ)ην

55. With the -(θ)η- ending, sometimes the θ is lacking in some verbs. Also, sometimes ε occurs rather than the lengthened η.

56. Aubrey, "Motivated Categories." See Allan, *Middle Voice*.

57. Fletcher, "Voice in the Greek of the New Testament," 314.

58. Fletcher, "Voice in the Greek of the New Testament," 307.

59. Taylor, "Deponency and Greek Lexicography," 171–73, although he seems to conclude that morphology is only part of the story, and function needs to be taken into consideration.

	Active	Middle	Passive
2nd Aorist	-ον	-ομην	
Future	-σω	-σομαι	-θήσομαι

Because, for economic reasons, formal redundancy usually does not persist in Greek, the separate middle and passive endings in the aorist and future should be differentiated semantically. The -(θ)η- ending, then, signals that the subject is the medium (i.e., the affected participant); however, in addition to subject-affectedness it now also indicates external agency, whether specified or unspecified. Some of the issue is caused by awkward English translations, such as "he was answered" for ἀπεκρίθη, or "he was come" for ἐπορεύθη. However, these can still be seen as true passives, with a translation along the lines of "was caused to . . ." or "was being moved to . . ."[60] In such instances, the external cause of the action can usually be found in the wider literary or even cultural context. For example, in Matthew 1:20 Joseph is commanded by the angel, μὴ φοβηθῇς (do not be afraid) to take Mary as his wife. The -θῇς ending indicates passivity, with the external agency found in the broader context: his discovery that Mary was pregnant and his not wanting to marry her. The translation "do not be moved to fear" could bring out the passive notion here. (For more on this example, see under "With Unexpressed External Agent" in chap. 3.)

An important verb in this regard is ἀποκρίνομαι. The aorist ἀπεκρίθη is frequent in narrative and is sometimes treated as a "passive deponent" (passive in form, active in meaning). However, the existence of middle -μην forms suggests that this should be seen as a true passive (he/she was moved or caused to answer), with the external cause usually found within the context. Within a dialogue, the need to provide a response is often the external factor (cf. John 3:1–15). This verb, when taking passive -θη- endings, can also take a further participant indirectly affected by the process that is the *recipient* of the process of answering.[61] In Matthew 14:28, Ἀποκριθεὶς δὲ αὐτῷ ὁ Πέτρος εἶπεν (But having been moved to answer him, Peter said),

---

60. O'Donnell, *Corpus Linguistics*, 372.
61. Fletcher, "Voice in the Greek of the New Testament," 319–20.

the passive ending -θεὶς indicates the subject is the medium and that there is an external cause of answering (he was moved to answer). But a further affected participant, a recipient, is indicated by the dative αὐτῷ. In fact, the very semantics of the verb ἀποκρίνομαι seem to require a recipient, someone "to whom the process is directed."[62] Alternatively, this could be an example where the -(θ)η- ending is taking over the middle voice, with the passive voice ending better suited to this type of verb.

Conclusion

This chapter has argued that a fruitful linguistic model for understanding the Greek voice system can be found in SFL and Halliday's treatment of the transitivity system and ergativity. In particular, ergativity focuses on the issue of causality: Does the cause of the action of a verb come from within or without? That is, is the cause of the action internal to the verbal process or external to it? On the basis of this notion of ergativity, this work has suggested that the primary defining feature of voice in Greek is causality. That is, voice is primarily a causality system in Greek. This then affects the role of the subject, whether it is the initiator and direct cause of the action, or whether it is the recipient or affected participant, the medium, in the clause. Voice is to be distinguished from transitivity and intransitivity, though related in that it asks the question of the relationship of the participants to the verbal process, but in terms of causality and agency. Thus, voice in Greek indicates the author's decision, by the selection of a particular tense form, to indicate the relationship of the subject to the action in terms of causality and agency.

I have argued above that the Greek of the New Testament can be seen as essentially a three-voice system, which can be differentiated along the lines of portrayals of causality, and morphologically in the aorist and future tense forms with the -(θ)η- endings. Therefore, the active voice form indicates direct causality and the subject as direct agent. With the choice of the active voice form, the least heavily weighted form semantically, the author chooses to portray the

62. Fletcher, "Voice in the Greek of the New Testament," 321.

action as directly initiated or caused by the grammatical subject. Such clauses with active verb constructions can take an additional participant (goal), or in terms of ergativity, the medium or affected participant, in the form of a direct object (transitive). Or the clause may contain no medium or goal of the process (intransitive). For the passive verb, the author chooses to portray cause as indirect; that is, it is external to the S + V nucleus. The external agent that initiates the process may be unexpressed or expressed. If expressed, it will be in the form of a prepositional phrase that is on the periphery of the S + V complex. With the passive voice, the subject functions as the medium, the affected element in the clause.

There has been much discussion and misunderstanding of the middle voice in Greek. For English speakers, some of this misunderstanding arises from the fact that English does not possess a middle voice (only active and passive). Like the active and passive, the middle voice in Greek indicates a particular portrayal of causality, and the subject then functions in a particular way. With the middle voice, causality is internal to the process; it is attributed to the S + V complex. There is no direct or external agent that initiates the action. Consequently, the subject functions as the medium, the affected participant, that is involved in some way in the process but is not portrayed as the agent (as with the active voice). Causality arises within the medium and verb together. In this way, the passive and middle voices are related, in that the grammatical subject functions as the medium (the affected participant) in both cases. However, what distinguishes the two voices is the level of causality portrayed: the passive voice indicates external causality, and the middle internal causality (ergativity). Understood in this way, there is no need to posit a separate category of "deponent" verbs (verbs with a mismatch of form and meaning—that is, "middle in form, but active in meaning"). Such verbs due to their lexical meaning have only middle endings, since the meaning of the verbs lexically indicates self-engendered causality, and therefore they lend themselves to taking only middle forms.

3

The Three Voices
in New Testament Greek

We have argued that the category of voice in New Testament Greek concerns the relationship of the grammatical subject to the verb in terms of causality and agency. Each voice—active, passive, and middle—represents a different morphologically based perspective on this relationship.[1] We have also argued that the voices stand in systemic relationship to each other, exhibiting a system of choices based on the role of the subject in relationship to causality and agency. The two main choices are between direct (active) and indirect causality, with a further choice in indirect causality between internal (middle) and external (passive) causality.

The following section on voice will treat the semantics of each of the voices in the Greek of the New Testament and their grammatical functions in light of the preceding discussion. It will also pay attention to their relationship to each other in terms of systemic choice and interpretive significance. For example, why would an author choose a passive voice over an active form (when there is a choice)? Regarding the middle and passive voices, attention will also be devoted to the concept of *deponency* and its validity for handling a particular group of verbs in New Testament Greek, verbs that exhibit

1. See Fletcher, "Voice in the Greek of the New Testament," 290.

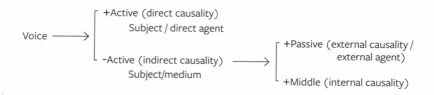

Figure 3.1

only middle/passive endings, as well as its function within the voice system. There has been much discussion recently on this issue, and this discussion will inform the following study. All of the treatment of the Greek voices and their functions will be illustrated by a sampling of examples from the Greek New Testament.

The Active Voice

The active voice in Greek is by far the most common of the three voices in the New Testament. The active voice is found some 20,697 times in the Greek New Testament. Therefore, distributionally it is unmarked and the least weighted of the voices semantically, in comparison to the middle and passive voices.

Distribution of Voice in the New Testament

Active voice	20,697
Passive voice	3,932
Middle voice	3,500

The active voice in Greek is probably the least misunderstood voice, being somewhat similar to its English counterpart. By choosing the active voice, the author chooses to portray causality and its relation to the subject in a particular way: +direct causality +subject / direct agent. By choice of the active verb the author chooses to portray the grammatical subject as agent (thus the "agentive voice"). That is, the active voice emphasizes the grammatical subject as the cause, or the energy source, that brings about or initiates the action or the state of the verb in a clause.[2] In terms of causality, the active voice indicates direct causality, where the subject (grammatically usually expressed in the nominative case, unless implied)[3] of the verb within the S + V complex is the direct cause or agent of the action of the verbal process. Hence, grammatical subject and agent converge at this point. Active verbs in Greek may take an object or not; that is, the active voice can occur with transitive or intransitive verbs.

Transitive Clauses

As mentioned above, voice is distinct from (though not completely unrelated to) the concept of transitivity and intransitivity in verbs. The active voice can occur in either type of construction. The question is whether the verbal process extends its action to another participant, the *goal* of the action, or grammatically, the direct object. Instances of this use of the active voice are not difficult to find in the Greek New Testament.

> Οἱ δὲ ἀρχιερεῖς καὶ οἱ πρεσβύτεροι ἔπεισαν τοὺς ὄχλους ἵνα αἰτήσωνται τὸν Βαραββᾶν. (Matt. 27:20)
>
> And the chief priests and the elders *persuaded* the crowds to ask for Barabbas.

> Σοφίαν δὲ λαλοῦμεν ἐν τοῖς τελείοις. (1 Cor. 2:6)
>
> But we *speak* wisdom among the mature [with an implied subject].

> Παιδία, μηδεὶς πλανάτω ὑμᾶς. (1 John 3:7)
>
> Children, no one *should lead* you *astray* [active voice with a third-person imperative].

2. "The subject acts as the original energy source, startpoint, and cause of a verbal process. . . . Causality is the output of energy that resides in the Agent" (Fletcher, "Voice in the Greek of the New Testament," 202).

3. Due to its inflectional nature, Greek does not require an expressed grammatical subject in its clause, but can indicate the subject in the verb's personal ending itself (βλέπω, I see). It also does not grammaticalize the subject in participle or infinitive constructions (unless one considers the accusative with the infinitive as the true subject), though the subject is usually inferable from the context.

καὶ ἐμνημόνευσεν ὁ θεὸς τὰ ἀδικήματα αὐτῆς. (Rev. 18:5)

And God *remembered* her injustices.

In all of the above cases, the active voice portrays the subject as the initiator or direct cause/agent of the action. The action then extends beyond the subject to an additional participant, the goal or object of the process. Some verbs can be "three-place" verbs with an additional participant slot, which is filled with a recipient of the action in the form of an indirect object, usually indicated in Greek with a substantive in the dative case.

σὺ ἂν ᾔτησας αὐτὸν καὶ ἔδωκεν ἄν <u>σοι</u> ὕδωρ ζῶν. (John 4:10)

You would have asked him and he would *have given* <u>to you</u> the living water.

> The second part of the clause extends the action beyond the implied subject/agent in an active voice construction to another participant, but also to a third participant, a recipient in the form of a dative indirect object.

Χαίρωμεν καὶ ἀγαλλιῶμεν καὶ δώσωμεν τὴν δόξαν <u>αὐτῷ</u>. (Rev. 19:7)

Let us rejoice and be glad and *give* glory <u>to him</u>.

> In this example, the last of three subjunctive verbs in the active voice includes a third participant, who functions as the recipient of the action (indirect object) in the dative case (αὐτῷ).

Intransitive Clauses

The active voice can also be found in clauses that are intransitive; that is, the action does not extend to an additional participant, a goal or object. The grammatical subject still functions as the agent or initiator of the action of the verbal process.

Μετὰ δὲ ταύτας τὰς ἡμέρας συνέλαβεν Ἐλισάβετ ἡ γυνὴ αὐτοῦ. (Luke 1:24)

And after these days Elizabeth his wife *conceived*.

> Here the active verb is intransitive and does not extend its
> action to another participant, an object or goal. Rather,
> the verbal action is modified by a prepositional phrase
> that communicates a temporal idea ("after these days").

καὶ προέκοπτον ἐν τῷ Ἰουδαϊσμῷ ὑπὲρ πολλοὺς συνηλικιώτας ἐν
τῷ γένει μου. (Gal. 1:14)

And I *was advancing* in Judaism beyond many contemporaries
in my generation.

> The implied subject of the first-person verb is clearly Paul
> (see Gal. 1:1), and the active verb does not extend the
> process to another participant. Instead, the verbal process
> is modified by three adjunct prepositional phrases that
> indicate sphere (ἐν τῷ Ἰουδαϊσμῷ), position (ὑπὲρ πολλοὺς
> συνηλικιώτας), and location or time (ἐν τῷ γένει μου).

Πάντων δὲ τὸ τέλος ἤγγικεν. (1 Pet. 4:7)

But the end of all things *is near.*

> The verb ἤγγικεν carries an intransitive meaning and does
> not take an object.

καὶ τὰ τέσσαρα ζῷα ἔλεγον· ἀμήν. καὶ οἱ πρεσβύτεροι ἔπεσαν καὶ
προσεκύνησαν. (Rev. 5:14)

And the four living creatures said, "Amen." And the elders *fell*
and they *worshiped.*

> The first verb (ἔπεσαν) is intransitive in meaning and
> does not take an object to complete it. The second verb
> (προσεκύνησαν) can take an object (the object of worship)
> but here is left unspecified, with the object easily supplied
> from the context (God and the Lamb on the throne).

Exegetical Significance

What function does the choice of the active voice form play in
one's exegesis? The active voice focuses on the subject as initiating or

causing the action (direct causality). It is the most common and hence unmarked voice form. Clauses that have more than one participant (a subject and an object), where the action is transferred from one participant to another, tend to have a higher level of transitivity[4] and therefore carry more prominence than clauses with only one participant (intransitive). Of course, other items can function to lend prominence (verbal aspect, conjunctions, person, extensive modification, etc.) to a clause.[5] Since the active is the most commonly used voice form in the New Testament, more important than the use of the active voice is departure from the active to the passive or middle (see below).

The Passive Voice

Distributionally, the passive voice is the next most common in usage, though falling far short of the number of occurrences of the active voice, and occurring only slightly more frequently than the middle voice (see "Distribution of Voice in the New Testament" above). The passive voice occurs about 3,932 times in the Greek New Testament in finite and nonfinite verb forms. By choosing the passive voice form, the author chooses to encode causality and the subject in a specific way: +indirect causality/external agency +subject/medium. With the choice of a nonactive voice, the author chooses to portray the action as indirectly caused and the subject as *medium*—that is, the entity affected by the action of the verb. The action is realized in the subject; hence, it functions as the medium. In prototypical passive voice constructions, the *patient* (direct object in an active construction) is promoted to the grammatical subject, and the *agent* (subject in an active construction) becomes an adjunct when expressed (prepositional phrase) or is implied.[6] That is, verbs in passive constructions are monovalent. The function of the subject as medium is indicated not by the formal ending of the nominal subject but by the voice form attached to the

---

4. Hopper and Thompson, "Transitivity in Grammar and Discourse."
5. See Mathewson and Emig, *Intermediate Greek Grammar*, 277–85, for some of these.
6. Zúñiga and Kittilä, *Grammatical Voice*, 83.

verb. "The subject in this role becomes the host and final embodiment of the process in which the process comes to its realization."[7] Within this choice to portray indirect causality and the subject as medium, the author must then choose either external causality and external agency (passive), or internal causality (middle). The former choice, the choice to express causality and agency indirectly and externally, is grammaticalized in the passive voice form. That is, with the passive voice the author signals that the subject is the medium, the affected entity, but causality and agency are external to the medium + verb complex, and are either unexpressed or expressed with an adjunct prepositional phrase that stands outside of the medium + verb nucleus.

In summary, with the passive voice the focus is placed on the subject as the medium, which is affected by or which realizes the verbal process, and agency is backgrounded in an external reference in the form of a prepositional phrase, if expressed, or within the broader context. According to Allan, "An agent-participant is conceptually present, but pragmatically deemphasized."[8] The following discussion will consider the use of the passive voice with or without an expression of external agency, along with the use of the passive voice with an accusative noun.

With Expressed External Agent

There are a number of ways to express external agency with the passive voice in the form of an adjunct prepositional phrase. Primary or personal agency is expressed with ὑπό + a nominal in the genitive case; impersonal agency is usually expressed with ἐν + a nominal in the dative case; indirect or intermediate agency is expressed with διά + a nominal in the genitive case. Cause can be expressed with the preposition ἐκ + a nominal in the genitive.[9]

τοῦτο δὲ ὅλον γέγονεν ἵνα πληρωθῇ τὸ *ῥηθὲν* <u>ὑπὸ κυρίου</u> <u>διὰ τοῦ προφήτου</u>. (Matt. 1:22)

7. Fletcher, "Voice in the Greek of the New Testament," 171.
8. Allan, *Middle Voice*, 41.
9. Cf. Porter, *Idioms*, 64–65; Wallace, *Greek Grammar*, 431–35; Mathewson and Emig, *Intermediate Greek Grammar*, 147–48.

And this all happened in order that what *was spoken* <u>by the Lord</u>
<u>through the prophet</u> might be fulfilled.

> The passive-voice participle ῥηθέν is modified by two ad-
> junct prepositional phrases, which distinguish between the
> direct personal agent of the act of speaking (ὑπὸ κυρίου)
> and the intermediate agent (διὰ τοῦ προφήτου).

Δικαιωθέντες οὖν <u>ἐκ πίστεως</u> εἰρήνην ἔχωμεν.[10] (Rom. 5:1)
Therefore, *having been justified* <u>by faith</u> let us have peace.

> The adjunct prepositional phrase ἐκ πίστεως indicates the
> external cause of the passive participle δικαιωθέντες.

ἵνα ἐν πᾶσιν δοξάζηται ὁ θεὸς <u>διὰ Ἰησοῦ Χριστοῦ</u> (1 Pet. 4:11)
In order that in everything God *might be glorified* <u>through Jesus</u>
<u>Christ</u>

> The passive voice indicates external causality, and there-
> fore the subject θεός functions as the medium, which is
> affected by the action. Indirect or intermediate agency
> is expressed through the adjunct prepositional phrase
> διὰ Ἰησοῦ Χριστοῦ. The ultimate agents of the process of
> glorifying God would be the recipients of the letter who
> "glorify God through their speaking and serving."[11]

καὶ οἱ λοιποὶ *ἀπεκτάνθησαν* <u>ἐν τῇ ῥομφαίᾳ</u> τοῦ καθημένου ἐπὶ τοῦ
ἵππου. (Rev. 19:21)
And the rest *were killed* <u>by the sword</u> belonging to the one seated
upon the horse.

> The subject οἱ λοιποί functions as the medium through
> which the process is realized. Impersonal agency is

---

10. I have followed the subjunctive reading for Rom. 5:1 supported by ℵ* A B* C
D K L as the correct reading. This is the reading accepted also in the Tyndale House
Greek New Testament (Jongkind, *Greek New Testament*).
11. Dubis, *1 Peter*, 145.

expressed through the adjunct prepositional phrase ἐν τῇ ῥομφαίᾳ. The assumed primary or personal agent in the context would be the rider seated on the horse, to whom the sword belongs. The use of the passive construction keeps the focus on the subject "the rest of humanity" and backgrounds the impersonal agent (the sword).

With Unexpressed External Agent

In instances where the external agent of the action is not specified but is still implied by choice of the passive form, the wider context will often clarify the assumed agent of the verbal process. However, at times the identity of the agent is ambiguous. In these instances agency is even further backgrounded, and the focus remains solely on the subject as the medium in which the action is realized. The fact that the present, imperfect, perfect, and pluperfect forms have identical endings for the middle and passive sometimes creates ambiguity for the interpreter. In such cases, "the overriding criterion is always what makes the best sense in the context."[12] Grammars and commentaries also often postulate a "divine passive," where God is the agent but is left unstated for theological reasons (i.e., to avoid use of the divine name). However, it is doubtful that this warrants a category of the passive, and so it should be dispensed with, since it is a theological and not a grammatical label. It is simply an example of a passive voice with unexpressed agent, the agent (God) made clear in the broader context.[13] Further consideration should be given to aorist and future verbs, which take a -(θ)η- ending. As already seen above, Aubrey has argued that -(θ)η- originated as a middle marker of spontaneous event types and later expanded to include more patient-like events.[14] Hence, verbs such as this are middles. It may be the case that the passive voice, indicated by the -(θ)η- endings, was taking over the middle usages. While Aubrey's view could be true of some verbs, if -(θ)η- endings mark passive voice, as argued above, then intransitive

12. McKay, *New Syntax*, 25.
13. It is doubtful that God's name is avoided in order not to mention the divine name. In many contexts where this supposedly occurs, God's name is mentioned close by in the broader context.
14. Aubrey, "Motivated Categories."

verbs such as ἀπεκρίθην, ὤφθην, ἠγέρθην, and ἐφοβήθην should be
placed in this category (see above). This is especially the case with
verbs that have separate aorist middle endings in addition to -(θ)η-
endings. For example,

| ἀποκρίνομαι | ἀπεκρινάμην (middle) | ἀπεκρίθην (passive) |
| γίνομαι | ἐγένομην (middle) | ἐγενήθην (passive) |

That is, with these -(θ)η- verbs the subject is involved in the action in
some way, but there is an external cause, though unstated. External
cause and agency can usually be found in the broader literary and
even cultural context. Possible translations for these instances are
"being moved to" or "being made to."[15]

ἄγγελος κυρίου κατ᾽ ὄναρ ἐφάνη αὐτῷ λέγων· Ἰωσὴφ υἱὸς Δαυίδ,
μὴ φοβηθῇς. (Matt. 1:20)
An angel of the Lord *was made to appear* to him in a dream, saying, "Joseph, son of David, do not *be moved to fear*."

> The cause of the angel appearing to Joseph, and Joseph's
> fear, can be seen in the context to be Joseph's discovery
> that Mary was pregnant and his decision to put her away
> quietly (vv. 18–19).

καὶ ὤφθησαν αὐτοῖς διαμεριζόμεναι γλῶσσαι ὡσεὶ πυρός. (Acts 2:3)
And divided tongues as of fire *were made to appear* to them.

> If the -(θ)η- is understood as passive, then something
> like "made to appear" is probably the force of the pas-
> sive voice. The agent that caused the appearance of the
> tongues of fire is left unstated and is not clear from the
> context, though probably it is God, given the quotation of
> an Old Testament prophecy that is being fulfilled in this
> event (see Acts 2:16–21), where God explicitly is stated as
> the one who will pour out his Spirit (v. 17).

15. O'Donnell, *Corpus Linguistics*, 372.

καὶ ὅτι ἐτάφη καὶ ὅτι ἐγήγερται τῇ ἡμέρᾳ τῇ τρίτῃ κατὰ τὰς γραφάς
(1 Cor. 15:4)

And that he *was buried*, and that he *was raised* on the third day according to the Scriptures

> The passive voice draws attention to Christ, the implied subject, as the medium affected by the processes. The use of the passive keeps the focus on Christ as the subject from the first clause: Χριστὸς ἀπέθανεν (v. 3). The agents of the burying and raising are backgrounded and left unspecified, though both could be inferred from historical and theological context.

ἀνάγκην ἔσχον γράψαι ὑμῖν παρακαλῶν ἐπαγωνίζεσθαι τῇ ἅπαξ παραδοθείσῃ τοῖς ἁγίοις πίστει. (Jude 3)

I had need to write to you, urging you to contend for the faith that *was delivered* to the saints once for all.

> The unexpressed agent of the passive verb can be supplied from the broader cultural context: those who first preached (the apostles?) the gospel to the saints.

τῆς πόλεως τῆς μεγάλης, ἥτις καλεῖται πνευματικῶς Σόδομα καὶ Αἴγυπτος, ὅπου καὶ ὁ κύριος αὐτῶν ἐσταυρώθη (Rev. 11:8)

The great city, which *is called* spiritually Sodom and Egypt, where also their Lord *was crucified*

> Again, the unexpressed agents can be inferred from the larger context. The first passive construction (καλεῖται) is a general reference to the identity of the great city: there is no specific person or persons in mind who call the city Sodom and Egypt. This is a general reference to how it is identified. The second passive verb's (ἐσταυρώθη) unexpressed agent can be inferred from historical and cultural references: those historically who put Jesus to death.

With Accusative Noun

While verbs in the passive voice are usually intransitive, sometimes passive verbs take an accusative participant. There are two possible explanations for this. (1) This phenomenon often occurs in cases where a Greek verb in the active voice takes two direct objects in the accusative. In a passive construction, one of the accusatives becomes the grammatical subject, and the other retains its accusative case.[16] The accusative case, then, may function as an accusative of reference/respect. (2) In some verbs the accusative case might have been a genitive or dative in an active construction: "He burned them *with a great heat*" (dative) (cf. Rev. 16:9, below). When this is turned into a passive construction, the dative case (expressing means) "advances" to the object slot and takes the accusative case.[17]

βαπτισθέντες τὸ βάπτισμα Ἰωάννου (Luke 7:29)
Being baptized with respect to the baptism of John

ἵνα πληρωθῆτε τὴν ἐπίγνωσιν τοῦ θελήματος αὐτοῦ (Col. 1:9)
In order that *you might be filled* with the knowledge of his will

καὶ ἐκαυματίσθησαν οἱ ἄνθρωποι καῦμα μέγα. (Rev. 16:9)
And people *were scorched* with a great heat.

Exegetical Significance

The passive voice indicates indirect causality and external agency, where the subject functions as the medium or affected participant. That is, the medium is promoted to the grammatical place of subject,[18] and cause and agency are indirectly expressed outside of the medium + verb complex. The passive voice is a departure from the

16. This is not common, but it is also not unusual in English in certain types of sentence structures. Active: "The teacher gave the *student* the *book*." Passive: "The *student* was given the *book*."
17. Culy, "Double Accusative." Cf. Mathewson and Emig, *Intermediate Greek Grammar*, 147.
18. Zúñiga and Kittilä, *Grammatical Voice*, 90: "In fact, most syntax-centered accounts of the passive domain have taken P[atient]-promotion to be both its defining feature and its main function."

unmarked active form, and an unexpected participant, the medium, fills the subject slot. In contrast to the active construction, focus is given to the subject/medium as the affected element in the clause in passive constructions, and the agent is backgrounded by being expressed in the form of a prepositional phrase, or left unexpressed. One of the important ways that the passive voice functions is to maintain "topic continuity." That is, the passive voice is used to keep the focus on the grammatical subject and to background the agent in a prepositional phrase, if expressed, as the external cause (the lack of expressed agent would seem to further background the agent). In Mark 1:9, ἦλθεν Ἰησοῦς ἀπὸ Ναζαρὲτ τῆς Γαλιλαίας καὶ ἐβαπτίσθη εἰς τὸν Ἰορδάνην ὑπὸ Ἰωάννου (Jesus came from Nazareth of Galilee and was baptized in the Jordan by John), the passive voice ἐβαπτίσθη keeps the focus on Jesus, who was the grammatical subject of the previous clause, rather than on the one baptizing him (John). In this way continuity of topic is maintained in the discourse.

The Middle Voice

The middle voice in Greek probably grew up with the active voice in the history of the language as the two primary voices, with the passive voice emerging later. The passive and middle voices can be distinguished based on the level of causality. Statistically, the middle occurs in the New Testament the least often of the three voices, being found 3,500 times in the Greek New Testament (see chart above, "Distribution of Voice in the New Testament"). This voice often causes the most difficulties for interpretation and especially translation for the English-speaking student, since although there are parallels in English to the Greek active and passive voices, there is no corresponding middle voice in the English language system. Furthermore, at times the active and middle voices will be translated similarly in English. This does not mean that middle *meaning* cannot be communicated at all in English but that it must be indicated lexically rather than grammatically by the selection of a set of verbal endings. There has been important debate regarding the meaning of the middle voice. Some of the debate has centered on whether the middle voice carries

a reflexive meaning as part of its semantics. Some grammars, however, recognize that the so-called direct or reflexive function of the
middle voice (translated with "himself/herself/itself") is rare in the
Koine Greek of the New Testament, and so it would be inaccurate to
highlight this as the meaning of the middle voice form.[19] Grammars
have consequently looked for other ways to define the Greek middle
voice. One way is to see it as a combination of, or "middle ground"
between, the active and passive. Therefore, the subject produces the
action, but then it refracts back upon the subject. That is, the subject is at the same time the producer and the recipient of the action,
or the agent and the patient of the verbal action. Others see this as
too simplistic and describe the middle voice as participating in the
results of the action in some way. Such definitions do not seem to
attribute any distinct semantic notion to the middle, but instead treat
it merely as a combination of the other two voices. This also seems
to assume that Greek is primarily an active-passive system, with the
middle somewhere in between, rather than seeing the passive voice
growing out of the middle. Therefore, recent research has pointed
to subject-affectedness, or the heightened involvement of the grammatical subject in the action as the main notion expressed by the
middle voice form. "The middle is the voice used to denote that the
subject is in some way affected by the verbal action."[20] According to
Porter, "the Greek middle voice expresses more direct participation,
specific involvement, or even some form of benefit of the subject
doing the action."[21]

As seen above, more precision can be achieved in understanding the
middle voice by defining it as part of the causality system in Greek.
By selecting the middle voice form, the author chooses to portray
causality and the subject and its relationship to the verbal process
in a particular way: +internal causality +subject/medium. In terms
of the subject, by selecting the middle voice the author chooses to
portray the subject as medium, as with the passive voice. The subject

19. Porter, *Idioms*, 67; Wallace, *Greek Grammar*, 416–17; Young, *Intermediate
New Testament Greek*, 134; Mathewson and Emig, *Intermediate Greek Grammar*,
148. Contra McKay, *New Syntax*, 21.

20. Clackson, *Indo-European Linguistics*, 143.

21. Porter, *Idioms*, 67.

as medium is affected by the verbal process, or the verbal process is actualized in the subject as medium. This is consistent with the notion that the middle indicates subject-affectedness. What distinguishes the middle from the passive voice in Greek is how causality or agency is portrayed. With the middle voice, which is the ergative voice in Greek, causality is internal to the process, residing in the medium + process complex, and there is no reference to an outside or external agent to the process, as with the passive voice. According to O'Donnell, "*Internal causality* is the meaning of the middle voice: the cause of the process is attributed to elements within the process itself in which the actor is involved."[22] This fits definitions of the middle that emphasize the heightened involvement of the subject, or subject-affectedness as the meaning expressed in the middle voice. The main point is that with the choice of the middle, causality is internal to the process itself, and the grammatical subject is involved in producing the action but is not portrayed as the direct agent or cause (i.e., active voice). As mentioned above, there may be an external agent in reality, but this is ignored with the middle voice, which grammaticalizes the subject not as a direct agent or an external agent but as the medium that is involved in the action in some way as the affected participant. The cause arises from within the S + V process.

The following section will treat the middle voice in transitive clauses, including the issue of how to deal with the accusative object, as well as intransitive clauses, and its importance for exegesis. It will conclude with a discussion of deponency.

Transitive Clauses

Many examples of the middle voice are transitive; that is, they include a "direct object" in the accusative case. Our first inclination might be to treat the accusative with middle verbs as the goal (grammatical direct object) of the action of the verb. However, normally the goal of a verb along the lines of transitivity in an active clause is the medium or the affected participant, which becomes the subject/medium in passive and middle voice verbs in an ergative system. So

22. O'Donnell, *Corpus Linguistics*, 371. See also Porter, "Did Paul Baptize Himself?"

how are we to analyze the accusative noun with middle verbs when
the subject is playing the role of medium and the affected participant? Fletcher, relying on Halliday's understanding of participant
roles in ergative constructions, is probably correct in treating it as
the *range*, rather than the goal or affected participant. That is, the
range, according to Halliday, "is not so much an entity participating in the process as a refinement of the process itself." The range
is an entity that "plays a part in the process not by acting or being
acted upon, but by marking its domain."[23] This insight can be applied to the accusative with middle verbs. As Fletcher states, "In
an ergative approach, however, a middle clause can have the exact
same clausal *structure* as an active voice clause, but *functionally* the
accusative participant is in a different kind of role to the process,
that of Range, and the subject . . . plays a different role, Medium."[24]
Furthermore, "This participant [accusative functioning as Range]
. . . is part of the process itself, adding to the meaning of the process
by specifying it, and helping to maintain focus on the experience
of the subject who fulfills the process."[25] Therefore, I will treat the
accusative nouns in a transitive clause with the middle voice not
as the goal or true direct object but as the *range*, which further
defines the process rather than a participant affected by it, since
the participant is already in the subject/medium of middle voice
verbs.

δὲ ὁ Πιλᾶτος . . . λαβὼν ὕδωρ ἀπενίψατο <u>τὰς χεῖρας</u>. (Matt. 27:24)
And Pilate, . . . taking water, *washed* <u>his hands</u>.

> With the use of the middle the emphasis is on Pilate's
> participation and involvement in the action of "washing
> the hands."

καὶ οἱ μάρτυρες ἀπέθεντο <u>τὰ ἱμάτια</u> αὐτῶν παρὰ τοὺς πόδας. (Acts
  7:58)
And the witnesses *laid* their <u>garments</u> by the feet.

23. Halliday and Matthiessen, *Functional Grammar*, 295.
24. Fletcher, "Voice in the Greek of the New Testament," 262. Italics his.
25. Fletcher, "Voice in the Greek of the New Testament," 262.

> The witnesses are the affected participants in the process of laying their garments. The "garments," then, are the range that further defines the process rather than the directly affected participant.

καθὼς ἐξελέξατο ἡμᾶς ἐν αὐτῷ πρὸ καταβολῆς κόσμου (Eph. 1:4)
Just as he *chose* <u>us</u> in him before the foundation of the world

> God is portrayed as the affected participant involved in the process of "choosing us."

Διὸ ἀναζωσάμενοι τὰς ὀσφύας τῆς διανοίας ὑμῶν (1 Pet. 1:13)
Therefore, *girding up* <u>the loins</u> of your minds

> The affected participant, or medium, is not expressed but is encoded in the verbal ending of the participle and is also indicated by the second person pronoun (ὑμῶν).

καὶ δοῦναι τὸν μισθὸν . . . καὶ τοῖς φοβουμένοις <u>τὸ ὄνομά</u> σου (Rev. 11:18)
And to give a reward . . . also to *those who fear* your <u>name</u>

> The middle participle can be understood in the same way as the previous example from 1 Peter 1:13. The subject is implied from the broader context.

Intransitive Clauses

The middle voice is often found in intransitive clauses, with no specified participant in the accusative case (range).

ἀπογράψασθαι σὺν Μαριὰμ τῇ ἐμνηστευμένῃ αὐτῷ (Luke 2:5)
To register with Mary, who was pledged to be married to him

> The middle infinitive emphasizes internal causality and Joseph as the affected participant. The process of registering is modified with an adjunct prepositional phrase.

εἴτε γλῶσσαι, παύσονται. (1 Cor. 13:8)

Whether tongues, they *will cease*.

> The use of the middle voice in 1 Corinthians 13:8 has at-
> tracted much attention. The middle form of παύσονται is
> often seen as contrasting with the passive forms καταργη-
> θήσεται/καταργηθήσονται. Prophecy and knowledge will
> be done away with by an external agent, the force of the
> passive. However, tongues will cease by itself, or will cease
> themselves. The conclusion drawn is that tongues will die
> out by themselves, and attempts are made theologically
> to locate the terminus of tongues somewhere in the early
> history of the church. However, this is a misunderstanding
> of the middle voice of παύσονται.[26] The middle voice indi-
> cates internal causality and the subject as medium as the
> affected participant. The verb παύω acts like a true ergative
> verb. When used transitively in the active voice it means to
> cease or stop something. But as an intransitive verb, and
> supported by the middle voice, παύομαι is ergative and
> indicates action internally caused. With the middle voice,
> the focus is not on how tongues will cease but on the fact
> that they will cease, with no specified agency. There may
> very well be an external cause, but the author has chosen
> not to indicate it grammatically and instead to focus on
> ergative causality and the subject as medium or affected
> element. The author may use the more marked middle
> voice form here to draw attention to tongues, which seems
> to be the gift in dispute in 1 Corinthians 12.

οὐκ ἔχετε διὰ τὸ μὴ αἰτεῖσθαι ὑμᾶς. (James 4:2)

You do not have because you do not *ask*.

> The middle occurs with the infinitive. For further treat-
> ment of the middle voice form in James 4:2–3, see below
> under "Exegetical Significance."

26. See Carson, *Exegetical Fallacies*, 76–77; Mathewson and Emig, *Intermediate Greek Grammar*, 151.

καὶ *κόψονται* ἐπ' αὐτὸν πᾶσαι αἱ φυλαὶ τῆς γῆς. (Rev. 1:7)
And all the tribes of the earth *will mourn* over him.

> The middle κόψονται does not here have an accusative
> direct object but is followed by a prepositional phrase (ἐπ'
> αὐτόν) that specifies the thing toward which the emotion
> of mourning is directed.[27]

In some cases the middle voice, when used intransitively, communicates a spontaneous process (see 1 Cor. 13:8 and παύσονται above). Such verbs are often causative in meaning in transitive constructions. These are the closest to ergative verbs in English (see above), where a transitive verb with causative meaning, when intransitive, is internally caused, and the object of the former now is found in the role of subject: "He *killed* them" versus "They *died*." Greek indicates ergative internal causality with the middle voice form, not the sentence structure. Here are examples in Greek:

ἀπόλλυμι (transitive)—kill (someone)	ἀπόλλυμαι (intransitive)—perish
αὐξάνω (transitive)—grow, increase (something)	αὐξάνομαι (intransitive)—increase
φαίνω (transitive)—cause to appear, show (something)	φαίνομαι (intransitive)—appear

ἵνα πᾶς ὁ πιστεύων εἰς αὐτὸν μὴ *ἀπόληται* ἀλλ' ἔχῃ ζωὴν αἰώνιον
(John 3:16)
In order that everyone believing in him might not *perish* but might
have eternal life

[τῷ λόγῳ τῆς ἀληθείας τοῦ εὐαγγελίου] . . . ἐστὶν καρποφορούμενον
καὶ *αὐξανόμενον*. (Col. 1:6)
[The word of truth of the gospel] . . . is bearing fruit and *growing*.

ἄγγελος κυρίου *φαίνεται* κατ' ὄναρ τῷ 'Ιωσήφ. (Matt. 2:13)
An angel of the Lord *appeared* in a dream to Joseph.

27. Mathewson, *Revelation*, 7.

Deponency

The issue of deponency in the Greek voice system has attracted much attention in recent scholarship.[28] As seen in the surveys of Greek grammars back in chapter 1, there is some debate as to the validity of the concept of deponency as applied to Greek verbs. As noted above, there are a number of verbs in Greek that exhibit only middle/passive forms and no active forms in their paradigm (see the examples below). Furthermore, they are often translated with an active sense in English. Generally, a verb is considered deponent if it appears only with middle forms. That is, the presence of active forms rules a verb out as being deponent.[29] Furthermore, as seen above, some verbs are deponent only in a specific tense (e.g., λαμβάνω is deponent in the future—λήμψομαι; γινώσκω is deponent in the future—γνώσομαι). The following is a very basic list of some of the verbs most commonly labeled "deponent" by grammars since they do not exhibit active forms:

ἀποκρίνομαι (I answer)

βούλομαι (I wish, will)

γίνομαι (I am, become)

δύναμαι (I am able)

ἔρχομαι[30] (I come, go)

ἡγέομαι (I count, consider)

λογίζομαι (I reckon, consider)

πορεύομαι (I go)

χαρίζομαι (I give)

For a fuller list of these verbs one can consult Robertson's grammar.[31]

A fairly popular understanding of deponent verbs is that they are "middle in form but active in meaning." Young states in his linguistic

28. See the surveys in Harris, "Study of the Greek Language"; Campbell, *Advances in the Study of Greek*, 91–104.
29. See Porter, *Idioms*, 71.
30. This includes all of its compound forms, e.g., διέρχομαι, ἐξέρχομαι, εἰσέρχομαι.
31. Robertson, *Grammar of the Greek New Testament*, 812–13. See also Friberg and Friberg, *Analytical Greek New Testament*, 811–16.

grammar that deponent verbs are "middle voice form but active voice meaning."[32] That is, deponent verbs represent a mismatch of form and meaning. Presumably, the active endings of these verbs were lost somewhere in the history of the language, and the middle forms have taken over the active meaning, or the middle endings lost their middle semantics. This perspective, however popular, has been significantly challenged lately.[33] First, there is little evidence that these verbs ever had active forms that have been "laid aside" (the meaning of *deponent*) so that the middle forms have now taken over the active semantics, or that the middle meaning was laid aside. More likely, something in the meaning of these verbs attracted middle forms only (subject-affectedness and internal causality). Second, the concept of "deponency" is an imposition of a Latin grammatical category onto Greek. Latin grammarians used the word *deponent* to describe verbs that were passive in form but active in meaning, and this came to be used to explain verbs that had only middle forms in Greek.[34] Third, given the discussion of voice in terms of causality above, it is possible to see the middle-only verbs as retaining middle semantics in their own right. The understanding of the middle as ergative, and indicating internal causality, effectively accounts for the verbs that occur only in the middle form, so that the concept of "deponency" is rendered unnecessary. Furthermore, I suspect that the typical definition of "middle in form but active in meaning" often reflects the English translation of these verbs, which often appear "active" in force. But English translation and the semantics of the English translation equivalent cannot determine the case, and our inability to perceive a "middle meaning" in these verbs does not mean that these Greek verbs did not retain a middle force. The current state of the discussion is summarized by Constantine Campbell: "While not all Greek professors are yet convinced that deponency should be abandoned, there is a consensus among most scholars working in the field that it should be."[35]

32. Young, *Intermediate New Testament Greek*, 135. See also Black, *Still Greek to Me*, 95; Dana and Mantey, *Manual Grammar*, 163.

33. See Pennington, "Setting Aside 'Deponency.'"

34. Taylor, "Deponency and Greek Lexicography," 170–75.

35. Campbell, *Advances in the Study of Greek*, 98. According to Taylor, "For Greek, then, what needs to be laid aside is the notion of deponency" ("Deponency and Greek Lexicography," 175). See also Pennington, "Setting Aside 'Deponency.'"

Exegetical Significance

As the least frequently occurring voice statistically, the middle voice can be seen as the most semantically weighty, foregrounding the notion of internal causality. It foregrounds the subject's involvement in the process as the affected participant. Interpretively, it is the most significant voice form for exegesis. The exception to this is so-called deponent verbs, better referred to as middle-only verbs, which have no choice when it comes to voice form. Since meaning implies choice, no specific exegetical weight should be attached to these middle-only forms. Where the author appears to have a choice, one can question why the middle voice form was selected. For example, in James 4:2–3, James's instructions to his readers on asking/praying alternates between the middle and active forms of the present tense of αἰτέω (αἰτεῖσθαι, v. 2; αἰτεῖτε and αἰτεῖσθε, v. 3). M. A. K. Adam, without justification, incorrectly concludes that "the active and middle voice of αἰτέω shade into one another, often interchangeably."[36] The fact that the two forms are alternated in such a tight textual space suggests otherwise. The choice appears to be intentional. The active voice form (αἰτεῖτε) simply portrays the subject as acting. The two uses of the middle voice (αἰτεῖσθαι/αἰτεῖσθε) occur in connection with the wrong kind of asking. The middle voice foregrounds in both cases internal causality, perhaps to emphasize the subject's involvement in and responsibility for the wrong kind of asking (lack of asking, or asking with wrong motives).

Conclusion

The above chapter has argued that voice is an important component in the verbal system in New Testament Greek and therefore can be important in exegesis of the text of the New Testament. While voice can function in a number of ways in various contexts, voice always indicates the author's perception of causality and the relationship and function of the grammatical subject to causality. Like other features of the Greek verb (aspect, mood, person, and number), the different

---

36. Adam, *James*, 77. Vlachos thinks that it may be because of James's conscious allusion to the teaching of Jesus in Matt. 7:7–11 (*James*, 132).

voices are indicated morphologically by the choice of a given verb ending. I have examined the function of the three voices—active, middle, and passive—in the New Testament in terms of their perspective on causality, illustrating this feature and its function in specific examples from New Testament texts to demonstrate the significance of voice. In analyzing voice in the Greek of the New Testament, interpreters need to move beyond the typical labels attached to voice functions by grammars (see discussion above) and focus on the perspective on causality and the subject indicated by the choice of a voice form, and what role it might play in a given context.

PART 2

MOOD

4

Recent Scholarship and Linguistic Insights on Mood

Introduction

As Stanley Porter notes, "The choice of attitude [mood] is probably the second most important semantic choice by a language user in selection of a verbal element in Greek, second only to verbal aspect."[1] However, given its importance next to aspect, it is somewhat ironic that less attention has been given to mood than even to voice recently (see below). As James Dvorak quips, in the treatment of the verbal system in Greek, mood has "basically 'been along for the ride' in this discussion."[2] Like voice (and verbal aspect), the mood of Greek verbs is indicated by the selection of a verb ending. In the Greek of the New Testament, the mood system exhibits a choice of four different mood forms: indicative, subjunctive, optative, and imperative. Furthermore, like voice, mood is perspectival in that it has to do with the author/speaker's conception of or portrayal of the action, not with the reality of the action itself.

1. Porter, *Idioms*, 50.
2. Dvorak, "'Evidence That Commands a Verdict,'" 203.

In the following three English sentences, while the semantic content of the sentence may be the same, there is a difference in the way the process is presented:

It is raining.
It might rain.
It should rain.

In the first example, the author/speaker simply makes an assertion about what is taking place. Whether it is actually taking place or not is a different matter. The speaker could be mistaken (it may be windy with dark clouds but not actually raining), or the speaker could be telling a joke or even lying. But the first sentence makes an assertion about what is deemed to be taking place. The second sentence indicates a process viewed as a possibility. There is potential for it to rain (perhaps this conclusion comes from a recent weather report). And finally, the third indicates a desire or necessity on the part of the speaker for it to rain (e.g., there are drought-like conditions), or a prediction on the part of the speaker when all the indications suggest that rain should be coming (e.g., dark clouds, smell of rain). This way of viewing the action in relation to whether the action is asserted as taking place, or not asserted as taking place but presented as a possibility or a necessity, is known as mood or modality. It refers to the author's conception of the action as it relates to reality. In English, as the above examples show, mood is indicated lexically by the choice of an auxiliary or modal verb (*might, may, should*).

In Greek, however, mood is indicated grammatically by the choice from a set of verbal endings that indicate the author's conception of the action as it relates to reality. As noted above, in Greek there are four mood forms, though the optative is "dying out" by the time of the New Testament and is only used in restricted contexts. Furthermore, mood is grammaticalized only in the finite verbal forms and, unlike aspect and voice, is not indicated in nonfinite verb forms (participles and infinitives, though these two are related in some ways to mood). The indicative mood develops across all the aspectual forms (aorist, imperfect, present, perfect, pluperfect), while the nonindicative moods (subjunctive, optative, imperative) are basically restricted to the perfective (aorist) / imperfective (present) aspectual opposition.

Recent Attention to New Testament Greek Mood

As already noted, the mood system in Greek is second in importance only to verbal aspect for interpreting the Greek verb. However, comparatively little attention has been given to it in terms of monograph-length treatments, with most of the attention coming from standard Greek grammars, and occasional treatments in paragraphs or chapters in books, of specific moods as a whole or in specific constructions.[3] A comprehensive treatment of the mood system in the Greek of the New Testament is still outstanding. The following is a survey of the treatment of mood in the same recent grammars that were examined for their treatment of voice above.

In his *Idioms of the Greek New Testament*, Porter devotes an entire chapter to mood in the Greek of the New Testament.[4] Porter defines mood as "the language user's perspective on the relation of the verbal action to reality." That is, "the mood forms indicate the speaker's 'attitude' toward the event."[5] Like verbal aspect, mood is indicated morphologically by the choice of verb endings. The moods can broadly be divided into two categories: indicative and nonindicative. The indicative mood, according to Porter, "is selected in Greek to grammaticalize an assertion about what is put forward as a condition of reality."[6] Porter is clear, following a critique of previous approaches to the indicative, that the indicative mood is a subjective choice on the part of the author, whether it has a factual basis or not. It concerns an assertion about what the author views as reality rather than indicating reality itself. The indicative mood is the unmarked mood used in statements and questions. The nonindicative moods,

---

3. See Porter, *Verbal Aspect*, 163–81; Boyer, "Classification of Subjunctives"; Boyer, "Classification of Imperatives"; Boyer, "Classification of Optatives." On the imperative mood, see Fantin, *Greek Imperative Mood*; Dvorak, "'Evidence That Commands a Verdict.'"

4. Porter, *Idioms*, 50–61.

5. Porter, *Idioms*, 50.

6. Porter, *Idioms*, 51.

by contrast, do not make an assertion about reality; rather, "the semantic feature grammaticalized by the non-indicative mood forms is one of 'projection' in the mind of the writer or speaker."[7] Porter then treats the three nonindicative moods in more detail.

The imperative is the mood used to direct an action. Porter discusses the imperative mood in relation to aspect, its occurrence in second and third person, and its relationship to the subjunctive mood. According to Porter, the subjunctive mood is the mood used to "grammaticalize a projected realm . . . which is held up for examination simply as a projection of the writer or speaker's mind for consideration."[8] He then considers the function of the subjunctive mood under the following categories of treatment: verbal aspect, commands (hortatory) and prohibitions, and emphatic negation. Unlike in some grammars, Porter does not distinguish formally or semantically between the hortatory subjunctive and the deliberative subjunctive (in questions). For the optative mood, the optative overlaps with the subjunctive, indicating projection, but with a further feature of *contingency*. It is infrequent in the New Testament, probably due to its semantic overlap with the subjunctive and its awkward formal paradigm, according to Porter. He then discusses the function of the optative under the following categories of usage: volitive (commanding, wishing) and deliberative (potential).

In his linguistically oriented intermediate Greek grammar, Richard A. Young defines mood as "a morphological feature that indicates how the speaker regards what he or she is saying with respect to its factuality."[9] He then briefly summarizes the semantics of each mood: the indicative mood represents something as factual; the subjunctive represents something as possible; the optative represents something as a wish; the imperative represents something as a command. The four Greek moods can basically be divided into factual and nonfactual moods. Young is careful to note that the moods express the speaker's perception of the action as it relates to reality, not the objective nature of the action.[10] Young treats each of the four moods in a fairly

---

7. Porter, *Idioms*, 52.
8. Porter, *Idioms*, 57.
9. Young, *Intermediate New Testament Greek*, 136.
10. Young, *Intermediate New Testament Greek*, 136.

standard way, with a list of possible functions of each mood. Thus, the indicative mood exhibits the following usages: declarative, interrogative, command, obligation, condition. Young notes that the last four overlap with the nonindicative moods. The subjunctive mood can be further defined as expressing a visualization of the action, or a subjective projection (see Porter above) of the action.[11] Young offers the following classifications of usage for the subjunctive: dependent clauses (which includes purpose, result, third-class condition, indefinite local, temporal, noun clauses), deliberative, emphatic negation, prohibition, hortatory. The optative mood, which expresses more hesitation than the subjunctive, can be used in the following ways: wish or prayer, deliberation, possibility. Finally, the imperative mood can be used to express the following: command, prohibition, entreaty, permission, condition, greeting. Young considers the use of verbal aspect with imperatives. He questions the assumption that the aorist is used only for specific commands, and the present for continuing action already taking place, or that prohibitions in the present imperative are commands to cease an action already begun. Only context can determine such nuances.

Kenneth L. McKay treats mood in his *New Syntax*, which focuses on the verb.[12] Mood is defined as "the function of the finite forms of the verb which indicates manner of presentation by distinguishing between simple statement of fact or intention, expression of will, wish, generality, potentiality, etc."[13] In a brief chapter, he summarizes the meaning of each of the four moods. The indicative mood is the most frequently occurring mood and is commonly used for statements of fact and intention. With secondary tenses it can be used for excluded wishes and conditions contrary to fact. The subjunctive mood, in independent clauses, expresses the will of the speaker or the subject of the sentence and can express an exhortation in the first person and be used in questions. It is more commonly found in subordinate clauses expressing purpose, apprehension, and (usually with ἄν) generality. The optative mood occurs in independent clauses to express a simple wish, and a possibility or probability. In subordinate

11. Young, *Intermediate New Testament Greek*, 137.
12. McKay, *New Syntax*, 53–54. See also pp. 73–117.
13. McKay, *New Syntax*, 53.

clauses it is used to express a remote condition and to replace another mood in a clause with a secondary verb form. The imperative mood is used to express a command, but also milder forms such as advice or entreaty. In subsequent chapters of his syntax McKay expands on these categories and the function of mood.

One of the lengthiest treatments of mood among intermediate-level Greek grammars is the chapter in Daniel B. Wallace's *Greek Grammar Beyond the Basics*, in which he devotes a chapter of fifty-two pages to mood in New Testament Greek.[14] Wallace begins by defining mood as a feature of the verb that "presents the verbal action or state with reference to *actuality or potentiality*."[15] Or in greater detail: "Mood is the morphological feature of a verb that a speaker uses to *portray* his or her affirmation as to the certainty of the verbal action or state (whether as an actuality or potentiality)."[16] On this basis, Wallace describes the four Greek moods as follows: indicative—certain/asserted; subjunctive—probable/desirable; optative—possible; imperative—intended.[17] He then divides the moods in two different ways: along the two poles of actuality (indicative) and potentiality (subjunctive, optative, imperative), and along the two poles of cognition (indicative, optative, subjunctive) and volition (imperative), though Wallace does not tell us what to do with these continua. He then concludes his preliminary discussion of mood by reminding readers that mood is affected by other features of language and intruded upon by lexical, contextual, and other grammatical features, though he thinks the mood meanings are still fairly stable.[18]

Wallace then treats the individual moods and lists a number of usages of each mood in the New Testament. The indicative mood is the mood of presentation of certainty. That is, the author presents the action as a reality, but this does not mean that the action is a reality. The indicative mood has the following usages: declarative, interrogative, conditional, potential, cohortative (command), with ὅτι (in independent clauses). The subjunctive mood represents an

14. Wallace, *Greek Grammar*, 442–93.
15. Wallace, *Greek Grammar*, 443. Italics his.
16. Wallace, *Greek Grammar*, 445. Emphasis mine.
17. See Wallace, *Greek Grammar*, 446.
18. Wallace, *Greek Grammar*, 448.

action as uncertain but probable, though Wallace says that this is an oversimplification. It grammaticalizes cognitive probability, but like the optative, sometimes possibility. He discusses the subjunctive under the following categories: (1) independent clauses—hortatory, deliberative (real or rhetorical questions), emphatic negation, prohibitive; and (2) dependent (subordinate) clauses—conditional sentences, with ἵνα, with verbs of fearing, indefinite relative clauses, indefinite temporal clauses. The optative mood, which exhibits fewer than seventy occurrences in the Greek New Testament, portrays an action as possible. Due to its rarity, Wallace concludes that when an author uses a form, such as the optative, that is being absorbed into another form (subjunctive), he uses it consciously. The optative has the following usages: voluntative, oblique,[19] potential, conditional. Finally, the imperative is the mood of intention, the furthest removed from certainty. It exhibits the following usages: command, prohibition, request, permission, conditional, potential, pronouncement, stereotyped greeting.

David Alan Black describes mood as the author's attitude toward the kind of reality in the action. Or in more detail, "Mood is the feature of a verb that a speaker uses to portray whether he or she has an actuality or a potentiality in mind."[20] The four moods can be boiled down to two essential viewpoints: actual and potential. Black makes it clear that mood has nothing to do with the reality of a statement but with the author's presentation or viewpoint. The indicative mood is the mood of reality. It is the unmarked mood that is most commonly used to make statements and ask questions. It manifests three main usages: declarative, imperatival, and interrogative.[21] The subjunctive mood is the mood of probability and is commonly used to express hope or desire. Black lists the following six usages: hortatory, prohibition, deliberative, emphatic negation, final (purpose), and content.[22] The optative mood is the mood of

19. Wallace describes this usage as the use "in *indirect questions after a secondary tense* (i.e., one that takes the augment—aorist, imperfect, pluperfect). The *optative substitutes for an indicative or subjunctive* of the direct question. This occurs about a dozen times . . . but only in Luke's writings" (*Greek Grammar*, 483). Italics his.

20. Black, *Still Greek to Me*, 97.

21. Black, *Still Greek to Me*, 98.

22. Black, *Still Greek to Me*, 99.

possibility, in contrast to the subjunctive, the mood of probability. There are two basic functions: voluntative and potential. Finally, the imperative mood is the mood of volition or intention. It exhibits the following usages: command, prohibition, entreaty, and permission.[23] A key feature in interpreting the imperative is the contrast between the aorist and present aspects. The aorist is the summary aspect, and the present portrays an ongoing process. Furthermore, the present imperative tends to be used with general precepts, whereas the aorist imperative is used with specific commands.

The intermediate grammar by Andreas Köstenberger, Benjamin Merkle, and Robert Plummer defines mood as "a morphological feature of the verb that indicates the author's or speaker's attitude (i.e., its actuality or potentiality) toward an event."[24] They then briefly define each of the four moods. The indicative mood represents something as certain or asserted; the subjunctive mood represents something as probable or undefined; the optative mood represents something as possible or hoped for; the imperative mood represents something as intended or commanded. Statistically, the indicative mood is the most frequently used mood, though they do not tell us what we are to make of this. Köstenberger, Merkle, and Plummer then discuss the four moods, repeating the standard labels to categorize their usages. The indicative can be used in the following ways: declarative, interrogative, conditional, cohortative, and potential. The subjunctive exhibits the following usages: (1) in dependent clauses—purpose or result, conditional, and indefinite relative or temporal; and (2) in independent clauses—hortatory, deliberative, emphatic negation, and prohibitory. For the optative mood, they suggest the following usages: voluntative, deliberative, and potential. The imperative mood demonstrates several usages: command, prohibition, request (entreaty), permission, conditional, and greeting.

In their *Intermediate Greek Grammar*, David L. Mathewson and Elodie Ballantine Emig discuss the moods and their functions in a single chapter.[25] They define mood as "the speaker's or writer's de-

23. Black, *Still Greek to Me*, 100.
24. Köstenberger, Merkle, and Plummer, *Going Deeper with New Testament Greek*, 199.
25. Mathewson and Emig, *Intermediate Greek Grammar*, 160–91.

cision regarding how to portray the relationship of a verbal idea to reality."[26] The indicative mood, then, makes an assertion about reality. The indicative mood is the unmarked mood form, the mood used when there is no special reason to use another. Mathewson and Emig are careful to note, "Whether the action or state grammaticalized by an indicative verb form indicates objective reality" is not indicated by the indicative mood itself but is "a matter of context, history, and the like."[27] The nonindicative moods, then, make projections or directions in relationship to reality rather than assertions about reality. Overall, Mathewson and Emig understand the meaning and relationship of the four moods in Greek according to their perspective on the relationship of the action to reality along the following scale:[28]

Assertion	Projection	Projection and contingency	Direction
Indicative	Subjunctive	Optative	Imperative

The indicative mood, which makes assertions about reality, can be used according to the following categories: declarative, interrogative, command, volitive (wish, desire), and conditional (class 1 and 2). The subjunctive mood makes projections about reality. Mathewson and Emig steer away from language of probability, likelihood, uncertainty, and so on, to describe the subjunctive mood, since any notions regarding the level of probability or certainty belong to the context and not the meaning of the subjunctive mood form. They then examine the subjunctive according to two broad functions: (1) in independent clauses—hortatory, deliberative, prohibition (μή + aorist subjunctive), and emphatic negation (οὐ μή + aorist subjunctive); and (2) in dependent clauses—conditional (class 3); purpose, result, content, and indefinite. The optative mood, like the subjunctive, indicates projection, but with the added feature of contingency. Mathewson and Emig find the following usages: volitive (wish, prayer, request) and potential (direct and indirect questions). The imperative mood is the mood of direction; it is used to express commands and

26. Mathewson and Emig, *Intermediate Greek Grammar*, 160.
27. Mathewson and Emig, *Intermediate Greek Grammar*, 160.
28. Mathewson and Emig, *Intermediate Greek Grammar*, 160.

prohibitions but also to request or grant permission. They discuss the relationship of the imperative mood to verbal aspect, presents, and aorists, disagreeing with common rules (e.g., present tense imperatives command an action already going on to continue). In addition to commands and prohibitions, they find the following functions of imperatives: entreaty (request), permission, condition, greeting, and interjection.

In a rather complex treatment of mood in Greek, Heinrich von Siebenthal in his *Ancient Greek Grammar* defines mood as the grammatical construction "used by speakers/writers to *express* how the 'situation' is meant to relate to reality, i.e., whether it is to be understood as *factual* or as *non-factual*."[29] He then introduces the reader to a number of linguistic features important for understanding mood. Linguists often understand modality according to three general categories: deontic, epistemic, and dynamic. *Deontic modality* refers to necessity with varying degrees of obligation or permission. *Epistemic modality* refers to the knowledge of the speaker/writer as the basis for the conclusion they draw about the reality of the action. *Dynamic modality* refers to the volition, possibility, and ability of the subject of the verb. According to von Siebenthal, the Greek moods cut across these modalities.[30] He then considers the range of functions of the individual moods, but also with reference to tense and aspect. Only the indicative form carries both tense and aspect meanings.

Von Siebenthal examines the indicative mood according to its function in main and independent clauses. In main clauses the indicative mood can refer to factual and nonfactual events. "Irrealis" events can be indicated with augmented indicative forms (aorist, imperfect, pluperfect), for example, in remote conditional sentences.[31] The future indicative also can express what is nonfactual, functioning as a command (obligation and permission modality). The indicative can also be used in subordinate clauses, occurring in declarative (with ὅτι) and conjunctive clauses. With the subjunctive mood verbs indicate only aspect, rather than tense. The subjunctive can also be divided into usages in main clauses and subordinate clauses. Its meaning is

29. Von Siebenthal, *Ancient Greek Grammar*, 345. Emphasis is his.
30. For discussion, see von Siebenthal, *Ancient Greek Grammar*, 346–47.
31. On *irrealis* and *realis*, see below under "Linguistic Insights into Mood."

basically volitional and prospective.[32] In main clauses the subjunctive is used *volitionally*: hortatory, deliberative, prohibitive, οὐ μή + aorist subjunctive for strong negation. In subordinate clauses, the subjunctive can be used in subject-object clauses to replace infinitives (with ἵνα), in expressions of fearing, and in interrogative clauses (indirect questions). The *prospective* use of the subjunctive can be seen in conjunctional clauses: temporal, purpose, result, conditional concessive, and manner. The prospective subjunctive is also used in relative clauses. The optative mood as well does not express any tense value, only aspect. It can also be divided into usages with main clauses and subordinate clauses. In main clauses, it is used to express an obtainable wish (deontic modality), a possibility. In subordinate clauses von Siebenthal sees the optative as functioning in conjunctional clauses, such as conditional statements, obliquely (indirect utterances, where it replaces the indicative) and iteratively (a repeated action in the past: "they used to/would . . ."). Finally, the imperative (deontic and epistemic modality) expresses obligation and directives. When negated, the imperative expresses prohibitions. Like the subjunctive and optative, the imperative does not express tense, only aspect. In both commands and prohibitions, the aorist is the unmarked form, frequently expressing a specific directive or prohibition, and the present is the durative form, frequently expressing general directives or prohibitions.[33]

What can be said by way of evaluation regarding how mood has been treated in the New Testament Greek grammars? First, most definitions are similar in that they define mood as a feature of the Greek verb that indicates the relation of the action to reality. Grammars for the most part also tie this to morphology; mood is indicated by the selection of a verb form. Furthermore, they are careful to note the subjective nature of mood: it concerns the author's attitude toward or the subjective portrayal of the action's relationship to reality, not the objective truth or factuality of the action. However, there are still some areas of ambiguity or disagreement among grammars in their treatment of mood.

32. Von Siebenthal, *Ancient Greek Grammar*, 352.
33. See the chart in von Siebenthal, *Ancient Greek Grammar*, 360.

First, most grammars repeat the standard labels that categorize the various functions of the moods without critically reflecting on their appropriateness. Second, although there is recognition that mood is a morphologically based phenomenon, there is still an uneasy synthesis between the form and the semantics of the moods. This can be seen in some grammars that suggest the indicative and nonindicative moods overlap with one another, so that, for example, the indicative mood can be used of potential action. For example, Wallace gives precedence to context and other features that can "intrude" on the meaning of the moods, raising again the question of the semantics of the moods themselves and the significance of the choice of one mood over another. Third, there is still some discrepancy and lack of clarity in the definition of some of the moods, especially the subjunctive. It has been defined as the potential mood and the mood of probability, volition, indefiniteness, and uncertainty. Much of this stems from failing to consider criteria for defining the moods according to their morphologically based semantics and often taking the most commonly perceived functions as somehow defining the moods. Fourth, apart from the works of Porter, Mathewson and Emig, and von Siebenthal, there is little reflection on linguistic issues and how they affect an understanding of the Greek mood system. There is often no consideration of the relationship of the moods to each other, and the system of mood and choice within that system; rather, the moods are treated in isolation. Overall, there appears to be little development in the treatment of mood across most of the standard grammars. Part of this may be due to the fact that little research has been done on the mood system in Greek in comparison with verbal aspect, and now also voice.

Definition of Mood

Mood, then, can be defined succinctly as "the speaker's commitment with respect to the factual status of what he is saying."[34] More specifically, in the Greek of the New Testament "the mood forms are used to grammaticalize the language user's perspective on the relationship of

34. Lyons, *Theoretical Linguistics*, 307.

the verbal action to reality."[35] If voice indicates the author's perspective on the action as it relates to *causality*, mood indicates the author's perspective on the action as it relates to *reality*. Three important conclusions can be drawn from this definition of mood for understanding mood in the Greek of the New Testament. First, mood, like other features of the Greek verb (tense, voice, person, and number), is indicated morphologically by the choice of a verbal ending. Mood indicates "morphologically-based attitudinal semantic features."[36] In selecting a verbal form, among other features (aspect, voice, person, number) the author is obligated to indicate his or her perspective on how that action relates to reality.

Second, mood has nothing to do strictly with the objective nature of reality. Mood is the subjective conception of the author as to how the action is portrayed as relating to reality. Wallace seems to miss this when he says that "even when there is a choice, the mood used is not always in line with its general force."[37] For example, Wallace claims that in wishes, such as "May God grant you . . . ," the use of the optative in Greek does not mean that the blessing is less likely to occur because the optative is used, rather than the subjunctive. At one level this is correct: the use of one mood over another does not indicate levels of certainty or likelihood of a process being objectively true or occurring. However, Wallace is incorrect when he says that a mood can be used in a manner that is not in line with its general force. Wallace views the moods as indications of the objectively true or false nature of the process, rather than as morphologically based attitudinal subjective portrayals of the relationship of the action to reality.

Third, the moods in Greek can basically be divided into two categories on the basis of the above definition: indicative versus nonindicative (subjunctive, optative, imperative) moods. While the indicative indicates the author's intention to portray the action as reality, all the nonindicative moods do not assert the reality of the action but represent portrayals of the action as potential or possible that are viewed as being further away from reality (e.g., projection, wish, intention).

35. Porter, *Idioms*, 50. For a similar definition, see Mathewson and Emig, *Intermediate Greek Grammar*, 160.
36. Porter, *Verbal Aspect*, 166.
37. Wallace, *Greek Grammar*, 447.

Linguistic Insights into Mood

Mood, or modality, has occupied the attention of linguists more generally, and some of these insights can be applied to mood in the Greek of the New Testament. As already noted, modality can be seen as the way that an author characterizes a situation in terms of its relationship to reality. Mood is the grammatical system in a language (e.g., Greek) that expresses those relationships.[38] According to F. R. Palmer, "Modality is concerned with the *status* of the proposition that describes the event."[39] More specifically, it is the status of the proposition as it relates the verbal action to reality. Though different terminology has been used to describe the moods, one way to distinguish the two basic moods is with the terminology of *realis* and *irrealis*. According to Palmer, "The realis portrays situations as actualized, as having occurred or actually occurring, knowable through direct perception. The irrealis portrays situations as purely within the realm of thought, knowable only through imagination."[40] Palmer's use of *portrayal* here suggests that this contrast should not be understood in terms of true versus untrue, since as we have already seen, the issue is not the objective nature or truthfulness of the statement but the author's portrayal of the action of the verb with respect to its relation to reality. Therefore, Palmer concludes that *realis* and *irrealis* should be understood in terms of assertion and nonassertion.[41] The importance of mood markings is that they depend not on what is factual and what is not but on "what is asserted and what is not asserted."[42] Thus, the primary semantic distinction in the mood forms is between assertion (e.g., Greek indicative) and nonassertion (e.g., Greek subjunctive, imperative, and optative).

Linguistics also employs at least two broad classifications of modality: *epistemic* and *deontic*.[43] Some would add a third classification:

---

38. Von Siebenthal states that "'Modality' relates to 'mood' in the same way as 'time (relations)/temporality' relate to 'tense' and 'aspectuality' to 'aspect'" (*Ancient Greek Grammar*, 345n53).

39. Palmer, *Mood and Modality*, 1. Italics mine.

40. Palmer, *Mood and Modality*, 1.

41. Palmer, *Mood and Modality*, 3.

42. Palmer, *Mood and Modality*, 4.

43. See Palmer, *Mood and Modality*, 7–10; cf. Evans, *Cognitive Linguistics*, 648.

dynamic. Epistemic modality "is concerned with the speaker's attitude to the truth value or factual status of the proposition (Propositional modality)."[44] Epistemic modality expresses the author's judgment regarding the certainty, likelihood, or possibility of an event taking place.[45] This can include making judgments on the factual status of the proposition, or giving evidence for such a judgment. Thus, declarative statements make an assertion without giving a reason for the assertion. At other times, a reason might be given for an assertion, such as what is based on something reported (He is said to be rich). By contrast, *deontic modality* (and *dynamic*) is concerned with "events that are not actualized, events that have not taken place but are merely potential (Event modality)."[46] It expresses the author's judgment regarding obligation, permission, or prohibition.[47] The most common type of deontic modality is directive or commands. Dynamic modality, then, expresses ability or willingness (e.g., He *can* run a mile in under four minutes).[48] Greek expresses dynamic modality lexically through the use of the verb δύναμαι (I am able) or θέλω (I want, desire), not through grammaticalization in the mood system.[49] The two modalities, epistemic and deontic, correspond roughly to the assertive (indicative) and nonassertive (nonindicative) moods in Greek. However, in another sense the Greek mood system cuts across the two types of modalities. Because the nonassertive subjunctive and optative moods express actions viewed as possible realizations, they can express epistemic modality. Yet because they can express commands and prohibitions, they fall under the category of deontic modality (see below).

M. A. K. Halliday in his presentation of SFL addresses the issue of mood and modality as part of the interpersonal metafunction of language (see above in chap. 2). According to Halliday, the interpersonal

44. Palmer, *Mood and Modality*, 8. Lyons understands epistemic statements as propositions that are known or believed (*Semantics*, 2:793).

45. Evans, *Cognitive Linguistics*, 648.

46. Palmer, *Mood and Modality*, 8. Lyons understands deontic modality in terms of necessity and possibility (*Semantics*, 2:823).

47. Evans, *Cognitive Linguistics*, 648.

48. For this description and example, see Palmer, *Mood and Modality*, 76–77. In this example, dynamic modality is expressed by the modal verb *can*.

49. See von Siebenthal, *Ancient Greek Grammar*, 347.

metafunction concerns the clause as exchange.[50] It involves the interaction of the speaker/writer and audience. "In interpretation of the
clause in its interpersonal metafunction as exchange and realizing the
tenor of the discourse, the clause is organized around the interac-
tions of the speaker and hearer. In the interpersonal metafunction,
the speaker assumes a particular speech role, as does the hearer on
the basis of the speaker's stance."[51] The primary system in the clause
as exchange is mood. The main types of speech roles, according to
Halliday, are two: (1) giving and (2) demanding. That is, a speaker is
either giving something to an audience or demanding something from
them. The other feature that cuts across both of these speech roles
is the nature of the commodity the author is giving or demanding in
the exchange: (1) goods and services or (2) information. When we
combine these two features, these variables define four main speech
functions: offer, command, statement, and question. Halliday illus-
trates this with the following chart:[52]

| | | Commodity exchanged | |
		Goods and services	*Information*
Role in exchange	*Giving*	Offer	Statement
	Demanding	Command	Question

These semantic choices related to speech functions are expressed
through the mood system.[53] According to Halliday, the mood element
in the clause consists of subject and predicator (verbal form). The
presence of both subject and predicator indicates the indicative mood.
Within the *indicative* mood, word order becomes important for determining two further speech functions. The order subject-predicator indicates a *declarative* clause, while the order predicator-subject indicates

50. Halliday, *Functional Grammar*, 68.
51. Porter, "Systemic Functional Linguistics," 20.
52. Halliday and Matthiessen, *Functional Grammar*, 107. See Halliday, *Functional Grammar*, 69.
53. These speech roles are also matched by the desired response in the readers: offer—acceptance; command—undertaking; statement—acknowledgment;
question—answer. See Halliday and Matthiessen, *Functional Grammar*, 108.

an *interrogative* clause. That is, the subject "is the constituent in indicative clauses that inverts with the finite verb to show whether the clause is declarative or interrogative."[54] The interrogative clause can further be divided into "yes/no" interrogatives and "wh-" interrogatives (e.g., who, what, where). The other major mood type is *imperative*, which is uninflected in the second person in English (e.g., "Run!"). The moods, then, express the four main speech roles: offer, command, statement, and question. For example, an *offer* can be expressed by an imperative (e.g., "Let's . . ."; "Let me . . .") or an interrogative offering "goods and services" (e.g., "Would you like me to . . .?"). A *command* would be expressed by an imperative (e.g., "Look!"). A *statement* would be expressed by an indicative/declarative (e.g., "She listened to the lecture"), and a *question* would be expressed by an indicative/interrogative (e.g., "Did she listen to the lecture?").

While Halliday and his articulation of SFL have highlighted the importance of speech functions and the moods that realize them, there are at least two issues with Halliday's discussion of mood that make it of limited application to the mood system in the Greek of the New Testament. First, it is not clear how the English moods correlate with the speech roles in Halliday's analysis. Second, the biggest hindrance to application to the Greek mood system is that Halliday's understanding of mood is modeled on the English language. According to Porter, "The formulation in IFG [Halliday's *Introduction to Functional Grammar*] seems to me to be based upon the clause structure of English, including its morphologically restricted set of English verbal forms (without, for example, a subjunctive form, etc., but which relies, instead, upon various modal indicators not found in, for instance, Greek). As a result, the speech functions are realized by syntactical configurations of the clause with limited modality (choices of mood forms), and hence the formulation above (in some instances extending the clause)."[55] As already noted, as with aspect and voice, Greek indicates its system of mood through a morphologically rich selection of mood forms, unlike English. Halliday's treatment of the speech functions depends on English word order to express them (for example, distinguishing declarative from interrogative based on the order of the subject and

54. Berry, "Clause," 107.
55. Porter, "Systemic Functional Linguistics," 26.

verb). Further, in English the forms of indicative and imperative are not differentiated, whereas in Greek they are formally differentiated. Halliday's division of mood in terms of indicative and imperative, with the former being divided into indicative/declarative and indicative/interrogative, leaves unaccounted for in Greek the subjunctive and optative mood forms.[56] Therefore, according to Porter, "The English MOOD system cannot necessarily be adopted for ancient Greek. Greek has a very different and in many ways much more morphologically rich verbal system. Greek does not have the modality system of English, but relies upon its more formally complex mood system. . . . This suggests both that Greek has a different lexicogrammatical system for indicating what Halliday labels MOOD, but also that Greek has its own means of developing different types of speech functions."[57] All in all, it would seem that Halliday's analysis of the English mood system is of limited value in understanding the Greek mood system and cannot be applied cross-linguistically, though there is some value in exploring the speech roles and their formal realizations in the mood system of Greek. However, in line with Halliday's discussion of mood, the mood system in Greek can be seen as contributing to the interpersonal function of the text.

Conclusion

Linguistics has added to the discussion of mood in important ways, especially in distinguishing assertive from nonassertive mood functions, and deontic from epistemic modality. It has also reasserted the importance of mood as the author's subjective portrayal of the action as it relates to reality, rather than the objective reality itself. Halliday has demonstrated the importance of mood in relationship to speech functions. However, some of the discussion is of limited value in that it is developed through analysis of English, rather than through the morphologically based mood system of New Testament Greek. The most important advance from linguistics for understanding the Greek mood system will be integrated into the remaining discussion.

56. For further discussion and critique of Halliday's approach to mood, and its value for modeling the Greek mood system, see Porter, "Systemic Functional Linguistics," 20–32.
57. Porter, "Systemic Functional Linguistics," 26.

5

The Greek Mood System

The following discussion will focus on the Greek mood system but will interact with some of the previous insights from linguistic approaches to mood and modality. As already noted, the fundamental distinction within the Greek mood or attitudinal system is between indicative and nonindicative moods, or assertive and nonassertive attitudes.[1] These two fundamental moods correspond roughly with epistemic and deontic modality. The assertive attitude is grammaticalized by the indicative mood form, and the nonassertive is grammaticalized by a series of nonindicative mood forms, labeled by grammars as subjunctive, optative, and imperative moods. Unlike in English, in Greek the indicative mood is indicated not by a configuration of lexical items in a particular order but by a set of verbal endings. As already seen above, the indicative mood grammaticalizes the attitudinal semantic feature of assertion and is used to indicate the author's intention to portray the action as reality (whether or not this corresponds to a factual basis in reality). The indicative mood largely indicates epistemic modality, making a judgment on the factual status of the proposition. However, unlike some language systems,[2] Greek does not indicate the evidence or reasons or manifest an evidential

---

1. Porter, *Verbal Aspect*, 167–68; cf. Palmer, *Mood and Modality*, 4.
2. See Palmer, *Mood and Modality*.

Figure 5.1

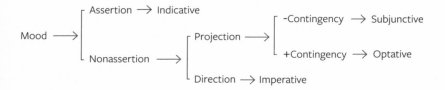

modality through its choice of formal endings, or levels of certainty or assertiveness, only manifesting one set of formal endings for the indicative mood.

Greek grammaticalizes nonindicative or nonassertive attitude through a system of choices among three moods, which will be further developed below. It will be demonstrated that the subjunctive mood grammaticalizes the semantic feature of projection or visualization. The optative mood overlaps semantically with the subjunctive mood by indicating projection or visualization but seems to carry the additional semantic feature of contingency.[3] That is, the action is seen as more vague, hesitant, and contingent on other factors. Finally, the imperative mood grammaticalizes the semantic feature of direction. It can be seen as the furthest removed from assertion in relationship to reality, in that it only directs an action. The relationship of the mood forms in Greek can be illustrated according to the systemic display in figure 5.1.

In a similar display, Porter also adds the further clause types of +interrogative and -interrogative in both the assertive and nonassertive moods.[4] Porter's own systemic display results in the following clause types and means of expressing them.[5] The initial terms indicate the semantic features of the clause, particularly the moods, but also whether they are negated (denial) or not (affirmative). The + and - indicate whether the feature is present (+) or not (-). The >>

3. A parallel might be the two imperfective aspectual forms in Greek, the present and imperfect, where the present and imperfect encode imperfective aspect, but the imperfect encodes the additional feature of +remoteness.

4. Porter, "Systemic Functional Linguistics," 27.

5. Porter, "Systemic Functional Linguistics," 28.

then points to the resultant speech function and clause type realized by these features.

+assertive -interrogative >> declarative statement (assertive clause with indicative mood form)

+assertive +interrogative +affirmative >> positive question (assertive clause question formulated so as to expect a positive answer, with indicative mood form)

+assertive +interrogative +denial >> negative question (assertive clause question formulated so as to expect a negative answer, with indicative mood form)

+assertive +interrogative +tonal[6] >> open question (assertive clause, with question tonally indicated)

+assertive +interrogative +elemental[7] >> τ-question (assertive clause, with one of the question words, with indicative mood form)

-assertive +projective -interrogative -contingent >> projective statement (noncontingent projective clause, with subjunctive mood form, as in hortatory or prohibitive use when negated)

-assertive +projective -interrogative +contingent >> projective contingent statement (contingent projective clause, with optative mood form, as in volitive use)

-assertive +projective +interrogative +tonal -contingent >> projective question (noncontingent projective clause, with subjunctive mood form, as in deliberative use)

-assertive +projective +interrogative +elemental -contingent >> projective τ-question (noncontingent projective clause, with one of the question words, with subjunctive mood form)

-assertive +projective +interrogative +tonal +contingent >> projective contingent question (contingent projective clause, with optative mood form, as in deliberative use)

6. *Tonal* means that the question is indicated by the tone or inflection of the speech, which is obviously more difficult to determine in a written text.

7. *Elemental* means that the question is indicated by an interrogative element, such as *what*, *who*, etc.

-assertive +projective +interrogative +elemental +contingent >>
projective contingent τ-question (contingent projective clause,
with one of the question words, with optative mood form)

-assertive +directive >> command (imperative mood form)

This proposal by Porter captures the major clause types, their speech
functions and semantics, and their lexicogrammatical realizations in
terms of the mood forms utilized.[8]

Jeffrey T. Reed offers one attempt to correlate the four Greek
moods with the four speech roles identified by Halliday (offer, command, statement, question). Understanding the four moods in light
of Porter's analysis (indicative—assertion; subjunctive—projection;
optative—projection + contingency; imperative—direction), Reed
suggests the following correlations, where the four moods cut across
the four speech roles:[9]

Indicative	Statements	Questions		
Subjunctive	Statements	Questions	Commands (hortatory)	
Optative	Statements	Questions		
Imperative			Commands	
[Future]	Statements			Offers

Though the indicative, subjunctive, and optative can all be used for
the exchange of information (statements and questions), the difference is attitudinal or the gradations of probability in the author's
perception of the action.[10] While Reed has demonstrated how the
Greek moods can function to communicate Halliday's four speech
roles, his suggestion is only preliminary, and more importantly does
not account for the fact that Halliday's analysis is English-language

8. According to Porter, "Semantics precedes lexicogrammar, and is mediated by
the speech functions that convey these meanings and are then realized in the language by means of clauses that perform the four functions mentioned" ("Systemic
Functional Linguistics," 24).

9. Reed, *Discourse Analysis of Philippians*, 82–83. Reed includes the future tense
form since it shares morphological and functional similarities with the subjunctive.
This chart is my own based on Reed's discussion.

10. Reed, *Discourse Analysis of Philippians*, 83.

based and does not capture the nuances of the Greek mood system. His suggestion that the nonindicative moods indicate gradations of probability in terms of the similar speech functions they express suggests the need for a more nuanced presentation of speech functions that takes into consideration these differences.

Therefore, Porter suggests the following modification as more adequately reflecting the speech functions and the structure of the mood system in Greek, resulting in the following ten speech functions.[11] These speech roles are part of the interpersonal metafunction of the language.

		Commodity exchanged	
		Goods and services	*Information*
Role in exchange	*Giving*	Open question	Declaration
	Projecting	Projective question	Projective statement
	Wishing	Projective contingent statement	Positive/negative question
	Demanding	Command	τ-question
	Enquiring	Projective contingent question	Projective (contingent) τ-question

As Porter concludes, "By means of clause types with their distinctive semantic features, this lexicogrammatical network identifies the variety of potential speech functions of Greek according to what can actually be expressed in Greek and what is being expressed in Greek by using such an expression."[12] He argues that this configuration is more adequate for Greek because it takes into consideration Greek's "rich mood-form morphology that results in a larger variety of formal or structurally based attitudinal semantic distinctions not possible in some other languages, such as English."[13] Porter suggests that his analysis is only preliminary, but it does capture the variety of speech functions and their formal realization in the mood system in Greek. Thus, it is an improvement over the categorization of Halliday and his usage by Reed. This way of thinking about the

11. Porter, "Systemic Functional Linguistics," 29.
12. Porter, "Systemic Functional Linguistics," 29.
13. Porter, "Systemic Functional Linguistics," 29.

Greek moods also constitutes an improvement over the traditional way of analyzing mood in most Greek grammars, where one finds lists of random functions (see the survey above in chap. 4). Such lists are vague and unprincipled in their criteria for categorization and discussion. The above discussion provides the basis for the following discussion of the mood forms in the Greek of the New Testament. Similar to the chapter on voice above, each mood will be considered, along with their different functions and a brief discussion of their importance for exegesis. Numerous examples from the Greek New Testament will illustrate the various mood descriptions and functions.

The Assertive Mood

As already noted above, the indicative mood in Greek can be seen as grammaticalizing the semantic, attitudinal feature of *assertion*. Von Siebenthal says that the indicative mood form is "unmodalized" and therefore does not express any modality.[14] But this fails to consider both the systemic relation of the indicative mood with the other mood forms and that assertion is just as attitudinal as the nonassertive moods. Through the selection of the indicative mood form, the author/speaker chooses to make an assertion about the action's relationship to reality (the other nonindicative mood forms will make no such assertion), putting forth the conception of the action as reality. As already noted, this is irrespective of the relationship of the action to objective reality. J. Gonda speaks in terms of visualization: "The ind[icative] expresses that the person speaking visualizes the process . . . as real or actual."[15] Previous treatments of the indicative mood as actually indicating reality are misguided and fail to recognize the attitudinal, subjective nature of all the mood forms, including the indicative. The indicative mood, then, encodes *epistemic* modality (the author's attitude toward the factual status of the statement) and is the mood form used when an author has no reason to use another;

14. Von Siebenthal, *Ancient Greek Grammar*, 345n53, 348. He seems to restrict modality to expressions of possibility, necessity, obligation, etc. See instead Palmer, *Mood and Modality*.

15. Gonda, *Indo-European Moods*, 3.

hence, it is the unmarked mood form.[16] In both primary and second-ary clauses, and across all the aspectual forms, the indicative mood occurs 15,618 times in the Greek New Testament.[17]

Distribution of Mood in the New Testament

Indicative	15,618
Subjunctive	1,858
Optative	68
Imperative	1,631

The most common function of the indicative mood form in the New Testament is in assertive or declarative statements.[18] One useful way of classifying the usages of the indicative mood (if indeed that is what we should do) is according to the clause types. I have slightly modified the proposal of Porter surveyed above, rearranging the functions that are expressed by the indicative mood, and arranging the different ways of expressing questions under the +assertive +interrogative function.

1. +assertive -interrogative >> declarative statement (assertive clause)
2. +assertive +interrogative:
   a. +affirmative/+denial >> positive/negative question (asser-tive clause question formulated so as to expect a positive or negative answer)[19]
   b. +tonal >> open question (assertive clause, with question tonally indicated)
   c. +elemental >> τ-question (assertive clause, with question expressed with one of the question words)

According to this scheme, the major division is between the two speech roles of statements (giving information) and questions (giving goods and services; demanding information).

16. See Palmer, *Mood and Modality*, 24–52.
17. Mathewson and Emig, *Intermediate Greek Grammar*, 161.
18. Porter, *Verbal Aspect*, 165–66.
19. Porter separates these two polarities (see above), but I have combined them as simply positive or negative sides of the same basic function.

Declarative Statements

+assertive -interrogative >> declarative statement

In declarative statements the indicative mood is used to make assertions about reality (+assertive) and is the unmarked mood form. It performs the speech role of giving information (-interrogative). This usage needs little illustration:

ἀπεκρίθη Ἰησοῦς καὶ εἶπεν αὐτοῖς· ἓν ἔργον ἐποίησα καὶ πάντες θαυμάζετε. (John 7:21)

Jesus *answered* and *said* to them, "I *perform* one work and all of you *marvel*."

> All the verbs in both the narration and the reported speech of Jesus are in the indicative mood, simply making assertions about reality or what the author perceives to have taken place.

παρέδωκα γὰρ ὑμῖν ἐν πρώτοις, ὃ καὶ παρέλαβον, ὅτι Χριστὸς ἀπέθανεν ὑπὲρ τῶν ἁμαρτιῶν ἡμῶν κατὰ τὰς γραφάς. (1 Cor. 15:3)

For I *pass on* to you of first importance what was also *passed on* to me, that Christ *died* for our sins according to the Scriptures.

> Paul makes a series of assertions in declarative statements with the indicative mood in establishing his argument for the necessity of the resurrection.

Positive/Negative Questions

+assertive +interrogative +affirmative/+denial >> positive/negative question

In an interrogative clause, the indicative mood (+assertive) can be used in positive (+affirmative) or negative (+denial) questions, which expect a positive (with οὐ[κ]) or negative (with μή) answer.

οὐχ οἱ πλούσιοι *καταδυναστεύουσιν* ὑμῶν καὶ αὐτοὶ *ἕλκουσιν* ὑμᾶς εἰς κριτήρια; (James 2:6)

Are not the rich *oppressing* you, and are they (not) *dragging* you to the court?

> The question (interrogative) indicated by οὐχ expects a positive answer ("Yes, they are condemning us and dragging us to court").

μήτι οὗτός *ἐστιν* ὁ υἱὸς Δαυίδ; (Matt. 12:23)

This *is* not the son of David, is it?

> The μήτι introducing this negative question expects a negative answer. At the least it expresses doubt on the part of the crowds toward whether Jesus really is the Messiah.

Open Questions

+assertive +interrogative +tonal >> open question

Open questions are indicated by tone, but this is difficult to determine in a written text, especially an ancient text. Other contextual factors must be relied upon to determine open questions with the indicative mood. Porter suggests at least the following two primary contextual indicators: "If the structure as a statement would contradict the clear statements of the text, or if it poses a set of alternatives, a question may well be indicated."[20]

ἐξ ἔργων νόμου τὸ πνεῦμα *ἐλάβετε* ἢ ἐξ ἀκοῆς πίστεως; (Gal. 3:2)

Out of works of the law did you receive the Spirit or out of the hearing of faith?

> This should almost certainly be punctuated as a question, since it presents two alternatives that cannot both be true in the context where Paul is arguing that justification

20. Porter, *Idioms*, 276.

is only by faith apart from works of the law. Therefore, UBS⁵, NA²⁸, and the English translations punctuate this verse as a question.[21]

An example of an open question follows:

ἢ ἀγνοεῖτε ὅτι, ὅσοι ἐβαπτίσθημεν εἰς Χριστὸν Ἰησοῦν, εἰς τὸν θάνατον αὐτοῦ ἐβαπτίσθημεν; (Rom. 6:3)

Or *are you ignorant* that as many as have been baptized into Christ Jesus have been baptized into his death?

> Romans 6:3 is an open question calling the readers to remember a key piece of information (introduced with the ὅτι) in Paul's argument. It is doubtful that Paul is making an assertion that the readers of Romans are ignorant.

τ-Questions

+assertive +interrogative +elemental >> τ-question

In an interrogative clause, the indicative mood (+assertive) can also be used in elemental questions (+interrogative +elemental). An elemental question is one introduced by an interrogative element in Greek (e.g., τίς).

τίς δὲ ἐξ ὑμῶν μεριμνῶν δύναται προσθεῖναι ἐπὶ τὴν ἡλικίαν αὐτοῦ πῆχυν ἕνα; (Matt. 6:27)

But <u>who</u> among you by worrying *is able* to add one span to his life/stature?

> This is an elemental question (introduced by τίς), which plays the speech role of demanding information.

---

21. Aland et al., *Greek New Testament*; Nestle et al., *Novum Testamentum Graece*.

The Assertive Mood (Indicative) in Secondary and Embedded Clauses

While the above examples are representative of the use of the indicative mood in primary (main) clauses, the indicative mood also functions in secondary (subordinate) clauses of different types, as well as in embedded clauses. The use of the indicative in secondary clauses makes an assertive statement in different types of secondary clauses frequently introduced by a conjunctive.

οὐχ ἡ γραφὴ εἶπεν ὅτι ἐκ τοῦ σπέρματος Δαυὶδ καὶ ἀπὸ Βηθλέεμ τῆς κώμης ὅπου ἦν Δαυὶδ ἔρχεται ὁ χριστός; (John 7:42)

Does not the Scripture say that from the seed of David, and from the town of Bethlehem where David was, the Christ *is coming* [embedded]?

ὁ γὰρ Μωϋσῆς οὗτος, ὃς ἐξήγαγεν ἡμᾶς ἐκ γῆς Αἰγύπτου (Acts 7:40)

For this Moses, who *led* us out of Egypt [secondary relative clause]

ὅτε δὲ ἡ χρηστότης καὶ ἡ φιλανθρωπία ἐπεφάνη τοῦ σωτῆρος ἡμῶν θεοῦ (Titus 3:4)

But when the kindness and love of God our savior *appeared* [secondary temporal clause]

ὅτι ἐτήρησας τὸν λόγον τῆς ὑπομονῆς μου, κἀγώ σε τηρήσω ἐκ τῆς ὥρας τοῦ πειρασμοῦ. (Rev. 3:10)

Because you *have kept* the word of my endurance, I will also keep you from the hour of testing [secondary causal clause].

The Assertive Mood in Class 1 and Class 2 Conditional Clauses

An important example of the use of the indicative in secondary clauses is the use of the indicative in the protasis of class 1 (assertion for the sake of argument) and class 2 (assertion contrary to fact) conditional clauses.[22] Though these two conditional-type constructions

---

22. For the labels for conditionals in Greek, see Mathewson and Emig, *Intermediate Greek Grammar*, 234–42.

are frequently treated separately, if verbal mood in the protasis (the "if" part of the clause) is our starting point in classifying conditional sentences,[23] then these two types of conditional sentences are related, with class 2 being a subtype of a class 1 conditional, since they are both marked by a verb in the indicative in the protasis. Class 1 conditionals have been the subject of much discussion. On the basis of the misunderstanding of the indicative as the mood corresponding with objective reality, class 1 conditionals frequently have been interpreted as assuming the actual reality of the protasis (i.e., real condition), so that it could be translated "since" to reflect this. However, grammars have now (at least in theory) moved away from this understanding, due to the fact recognized by most grammars that the indicative mood is the subjective portrayal by the author of the relationship of the verbal process to reality. Early research by James Boyer suggested that on the basis of context, 63 percent of all class 1 conditional sentences were either false in reality (12 percent), or undetermined as to whether true or false (51 percent).[24] That is, class 1 conditionals only assume the truth or reality of the protasis. Semantically, class 1 conditions make an assertion about reality in the protasis for the sake of the argument. This is consistent with the understanding of the indicative as the author's subjective portrayal of the action in relationship to reality, as argued above. Whether the protasis is true or not depends on other contextual, historical, or theological factors, not the grammar of the clause. Often the class 1 conditional functions rhetorically to move the reader to draw the appropriate conclusion.[25] That class 1 conditions do not assume the objective reality of the protasis (and hence should be translated "since") can be seen from examples where conflicting alternatives are both presented with class 1 conditional statements. For example, in Jesus's defense of his casting out demons in Matthew 12, in the face of accusations by the Pharisees that he does so under Satan's power, Jesus replies with two class 1 conditional statements:

23. See Porter, *Verbal Aspect*, 291–320; Robertson and Davis, *New Short Grammar*, 350.
24. Boyer, "First Class Conditions." See also Mathewson and Emig, *Intermediate Greek Grammar*, 235–38; Carson, *Exegetical Fallacies*, 77–78.
25. Mathewson and Emig, *Intermediate Greek Grammar*, 237–38.

καὶ εἰ ἐγὼ ἐν Βεελζεβοὺλ ἐκβάλλω τὰ δαιμόνια, οἱ υἱοὶ ὑμῶν ἐν τίνι ἐκβάλλουσιν; διὰ τοῦτο αὐτοὶ κριταὶ ἔσονται ὑμῶν. εἰ δὲ ἐν πνεύματι θεοῦ ἐγὼ ἐκβάλλω τὰ δαιμόνια, ἄρα ἔφθασεν ἐφ' ὑμᾶς ἡ βασιλεία τοῦ θεοῦ. (Matt. 12:27–28)

And if I *cast out* demons by Beelzebul, by whom do your sons cast them out? Because of this they will be your judges. But if I *cast out* demons by the Spirit of God, then the kingdom of God has come upon you.

> Matthew's account of Jesus's speech poses alternative scenarios to the Pharisees, using class 1 conditional sentences, with εἰ + indicative in the protases of both instances. Yet understanding them as presenting objective reality, and hence translating them "since," makes no sense here. It cannot be true that Jesus casts out demons both by Beelzebul and by the Spirit of God. However, both make sense when the class 1 conditional is only assuming the truth or reality of the protasis for the sake of the argument. Both conditional statements make an assertion for the sake of the argument, leaving the readers to draw the appropriate conclusion.

Εἰ δὲ Χριστὸς κηρύσσεται ὅτι ἐκ νεκρῶν ἐγήγερται, πῶς λέγουσιν ἐν ὑμῖν τινες ὅτι ἀνάστασις νεκρῶν οὐκ ἔστιν; (1 Cor. 15:12)

But if Christ *is preached*, that he is raised from the dead, how are some of you saying that there is no resurrection of the dead?

> The preaching of Christ is asserted for the sake of argument (the truth of the statement must be determined on contextual grounds) in order to point out the absurdity of what is said in the question that follows.

As noted above, class 2 conditionals should be seen as a subset of the class 1 conditional, due to the fact that both are marked by an indicative verb form (with εἰ) in the protasis. The other elements of a class 2 conditional are (1) ἄν in the apodosis and (2) secondary tense forms (aorist, imperfect) in the protasis and apodosis. The class 2 conditional is the contrary-to-fact condition. In this class of conditional, the protasis contains an assertion that is regarded as contrary to fact, so that the apodosis remains unfulfilled. In the English sentence, "If she had studied, she would have received an A," what is asserted is that she did not study, so then the apodosis (receiving an A) remains unfulfilled.

εἰ γὰρ ἔγνωσαν, οὐκ ἂν τὸν κύριον τῆς δόξης ἐσταύρωσαν. (1 Cor. 2:8)

For if they *had known*, they would not have crucified the Lord of glory.

> The protasis makes an assertion that is regarded as contrary to fact. Therefore, the apodosis remains unfulfilled—they did crucify the Lord of glory.

Exegetical Significance

Given that it is the most commonly occurring mood distributionally, the indicative mood functions in primary (main) clauses to provide background information.[26] It is the normal mood to use for statements and questions. It makes assertions and posits questions that form the backdrop for statements in the nonindicative moods in primary clauses (especially the subjunctive used in hortatory statements and interrogative projective questions, and the imperative). It is also the common mood used in narrative to make assertions regarding what the writer wants to present as fact. Therefore, in Mark 5:1–8 all the main verbs are in the indicative mood. In Colossians 2:13–15 Paul makes a number of assertions in the form of declarative statements that specify what Christ has accomplished on behalf of his people through his death. Verses 16–19 shift to the imperative mood to direct the readers in the appropriate conduct. In other words, the directives in verses 16–19 are grounded in the assertive statements in verses 13–15.

26. Porter, "Prominence," 62: "In primary clauses, the indicative mood form appears to be the background form, since it merely makes an assertion about what is put forward as the condition of reality, without any statement as to its actuality."

The Nonassertive Moods

The nonassertive, or nonindicative, moods share the common semantic feature of making no assertion about reality (-assertion) and instead making projections about reality. As Gonda correctly concludes, "If we describe the verbal category of mood (such as it appears in Greek or Sanskrit) as a means of intimating the speaker's view or conception of the relation of the process expressed by the verb to reality, it will be clear that the main distinction made is between what the speaker puts forward as fact (whether it be true or not) and what he does not regard as such."[27] That is, the nonindicative moods share the feature of making no assertion about the verbal process as it relates to reality but operate in the realm of projection or volition. Thus, the nonassertive moods generally indicate *deontic* modality, referring "to events that are not actualized . . . but are merely potential."[28] However, in questions and projective statements they can indicate epistemic modality, in that they express potential or possible action. Within the nonassertive moods, there are different semantic shades grammaticalized by each mood. It may also be helpful to visualize the moods, in the order in which they are presented below, as each representing stages further removed from making assertions about reality (indicative mood).

Subjunctive (Projection)

The subjunctive mood is the second-most common mood in the New Testament, though far less frequent than the indicative, occurring around 1,858 times. There has been much discussion in the grammars regarding the semantics of the subjunctive mood form. The subjunctive mood has been variously described as the mood of probability, desirable action, or intentionality, or as representing an action as uncertain but probable (see the survey of grammars above). These various semantic approaches and labels, however, not only reflect only some of the usages of the subjunctive, but also sometimes confuse reality with the author's conception of reality, do not

27. Gonda, *Indo-European Moods*, 6.
28. Palmer, *Mood and Modality*, 70.

consider the relationship between the subjunctive and other mood forms, and do not get at the semantics of the mood that accounts for its various realizations in its contexts. Two proposals offer a more fruitful way forward. In his work on the moods in Indo-European languages, Gonda argues that the primary function of the subjunctive mood is *visualization*. "Its general function may, if I am not mistaken, have been to indicate that the speaker views the process denoted by the verb as existing in his mind or before his mental eye, or rather: as not yet having a higher degree of being than mental existence. The subjunctive, in other words, expresses *visualization*. A process in the subj[unctive] represents a mental image on the part of the speaker which, in his opinion, is capable of realization, or even awaits realization."[29] Building off the work of Gonda, Porter suggests that the semantic feature that best characterizes the subjunctive mood is *projection*. Porter thinks that Gonda's notion of visualization too closely suggests the creating of an image of the process in the mind. Therefore, Porter proposes the term *projection* as more adequately capturing the semantics of the subjunctive mood. The subjunctive thus could be defined as "the form . . . used to grammaticalize a projected realm which may at some time exist and may even now exist, but which is held up for examination simply as a projection of the writer or speaker's mind for consideration."[30] As one of the nonassertive, volitional (deontic) moods, the major unifying semantic feature of the subjunctive mood that takes into account its various functions is projection or visualization, where a hypothetical realm, capable of being realized, is presented for consideration. The action is only a potentiality or within the realm of possibility. Further notions such as probability, likelihood, levels of certainty of fulfillment, and so on, do not belong to the semantics of the subjunctive mood but are determined only by context.[31] Any further nuances belong

29. Gonda, *Indo-European Moods*, 69–70. Italics mine.

30. Porter, *Idioms*, 57.

31. "Whether the speaker expects this realization, desires it, fears it, orders or hopes it or whether he merely sees it before his mental eyes, is a matter of indifference. Any implications and specialization: wish, adhortation, deliberation, 'anticipation' depends on circumstances: context, situation, intonation, meaning of the verb, and in spoken language also on gestures" (Gonda, *Indo-European Moods*, 70). See also Mathewson and Emig, *Intermediate Greek Grammar*, 165.

to broader contextual considerations, not to the semantics of the subjunctive mood itself.

Rather than the hodgepodge of labels found in most grammars (see the survey above), the following rearrangement of the suggestive scheme of Porter above lays out the primary usages of the subjunctive. It breaks down the functions of the subjunctive under the broader categories of projective clauses and projective interrogative clauses.

1. -assertive +projective -interrogative -contingent >> projective statement (noncontingent projective clause, with subjunctive mood form, as in hortatory or prohibitive use when negated)
2. -assertive +projective +interrogative:
    a. +tonal -contingent >> projective question (noncontingent projective clause, with subjunctive mood form, as in deliberative use)
    b. +elemental -contingent >> projective τ-question (noncontingent projective clause, with one of the question words, with subjunctive mood form)

The function of projective statements and questions with the subjunctive mood form accounts for the use of the subjunctive in primary clauses. Grammarians usually label these as hortatory, prohibitive, and deliberative subjunctive functions. The notion of projection lends itself to the subjunctive functioning in a hortatory or prohibitive manner, expressing deontic modality. The subjunctive projects a state of affairs that is to be realized in the action of the hearers/readers, or is prohibited of them.

Projective Statements

-assertive +projective -interrogative -contingent >> projective statement

A projective statement uses a subjunctive mood form (-assertive +projective) in a noncontingent (-contingent), projective clause, such as in hortatory or prohibitive use when negated.

μὴ φοβηθῇς παραλαβεῖν Μαρίαν τὴν γυναῖκά σου. (Matt. 1:20)

Do not *be afraid* to take Mary as your wife [a negated second-person subjunctive].

χαίρωμεν καὶ ἀγαλλιῶμεν καὶ δώσωμεν τὴν δόξαν αὐτῷ, ὅτι ἦλθεν ὁ γάμος τοῦ ἀρνίου. (Rev. 19:7)

Let us rejoice and *let us exalt*, and *let us give* glory to him, for the marriage of the Lamb has come [first-person plural hortatory subjunctives].

πνεύματι περιπατεῖτε καὶ ἐπιθυμίαν σαρκὸς οὐ μὴ τελέσητε. (Gal. 5:16)

Walk in the Spirit, and you *will* never *fulfill* the desire of the flesh [strong negation with the doubly negated (οὐ μή) aorist subjunctive projective statement].

Projective Questions

-assertive +projective +interrogative +tonal -contingent >> projective question

The subjunctive mood (-assertive +projective) can be used in a deliberative sense (+interrogative +tonal) in a projective question. The so-called deliberative subjunctive should probably be seen as the hortatory subjunctive just put in question form.[32]

ἔξεστιν δοῦναι κῆνσον Καίσαρι ἢ οὔ; δῶμεν ἢ μὴ δῶμεν; (Mark 12:14)

Is it lawful to pay taxes to Caesar or not? *Should we give* or *should we* not *give*?

ἁμαρτήσωμεν, ὅτι οὐκ ἐσμὲν ὑπὸ νόμον ἀλλ' ὑπὸ χάριν; (Rom. 6:15)

Should we sin because we are not under the law but under grace?

---

32. Moule, *Idiom Book*, 22; Porter, *Idioms*, 58; Mathewson and Emig, *Intermediate Greek Grammar*, 167.

Projective τ-Questions

-assertive +projective +interrogative +elemental -contingent >> projective τ-question

A projective τ-question is a noncontingent (-contingent) projective clause that uses a subjunctive mood form (-assertive +projective) in a question (+interrogative) using one of the question words (e.g., τίς).

Μὴ οὖν μεριμνήσητε λέγοντες· τί φάγωμεν; ἤ· τί πίωμεν; ἤ· τί περιβαλώμεθα; (Matt. 6:31)

Therefore, do not worry [about tomorrow], saying: "What shall we eat?" or "What shall we drink?" or "What shall we clothe ourselves with?"

τί ποιῶμεν ἵνα ἐργαζώμεθα τὰ ἔργα τοῦ θεοῦ; (John 6:28)

What shall we do in order that we might do the works of God?

The Subjunctive in Secondary Clauses

The subjunctive mood (-assertive +projective) making a projective statement is also frequent in secondary (dependent) conjunctive clauses. That is, in certain types of secondary clauses, the author chooses to project a state of affairs for a variety of purposes.

Purpose/Result

ἵνα πληρωθῇ τὸ ῥηθὲν ὑπὸ κυρίου διὰ τοῦ προφήτου (Matt. 2:15)

In order that what was spoken by the Lord through the prophet might be fulfilled

ἵνα εἰς τὰ ἔθνη ἡ εὐλογία τοῦ Ἀβραὰμ γένηται ἐν Χριστῷ Ἰησοῦ, ἵνα τὴν ἐπαγγελίαν τοῦ πνεύματος λάβωμεν διὰ τῆς πίστεως (Gal. 3:14)

In order that the blessing of Abraham might come to the Gentiles in Christ Jesus, in order that we might receive the promise of the Spirit through faith

Here, two projective secondary clauses indicate purpose, with the second clause modifying the first one.

Indefinite (Temporal, Relative, Local)

Once more, these are not so much different usages of the subjunctive but fall under the category of making a projective statement in secondary clauses of differing types.

ὅταν ὁ Χριστὸς φανερωθῇ, ἡ ζωὴ ὑμῶν (Col. 3:4)

Whenever Christ, your life, *would appear* [temporal]

ὃς δ᾽ ἂν βλασφημήσῃ εἰς τὸ πνεῦμα τὸ ἅγιον, οὐκ ἔχει ἄφεσιν εἰς τὸν αἰῶνα. (Mark 3:29)

But whoever *might blaspheme* the Holy Spirit will not have forgiveness forever [relative].

οὗτοι οἱ ἀκολουθοῦντες τῷ ἀρνίῳ ὅπου ἂν ὑπάγῃ. (Rev. 14:4)

These are the ones following the Lamb wherever *he goes* [local].

Condition

The subjunctive mood is used in the protasis of class 3 type conditional statements, following the conjunctive ἐάν. Unlike class 1 (and class 2) type conditions, which make an assertion for the sake of argument, class 3 conditions with the subjunctive mood project a hypothetical state of affairs as the basis for the condition. Again, how likely or probable it is for the condition to be fulfilled is not part of the semantics of the subjunctive used in class 3 conditions. It is used when for various reasons an author wants to project a possible realm capable of realization. This, along with the nontemporal nature of the subjunctive mood form, also renders unnecessary categories such as present general condition and future more probable condition.[33]

καὶ εἶπεν αὐτῷ· ταῦτά σοι πάντα δώσω, <u>ἐὰν</u> πεσὼν προσκυνήσῃς μοι. (Matt. 4:9)

And he said to him [Jesus], "I will give you all these things, <u>if</u> you fall down and *worship* me."

> In the threefold temptation of Jesus by Satan in Matthew 4, the first two temptations are framed as class 1 conditions

33. See Wallace, *Greek Grammar*, 696–97.

> (εἰ υἱὸς εἶ τοῦ θεοῦ, vv. 3, 6). The third temptation is in the
> form of a class 3 condition. It is possible that the class 3
> condition with the subjunctive is used to express doubt in
> Satan's mind as to whether he could get Jesus to do this.
> Yet, it is also possible that the class 3 condition functions
> to foreground this temptation as the most significant test.[34]

ἐάν τις ἀγαπᾷ τὸν κόσμον, οὐκ ἔστιν ἡ ἀγάπη τοῦ πατρὸς ἐν αὐτῷ.
(1 John 2:15)

If anyone *might love* the world, the love of the Father is not in
them.

> At times, within the broader discourse context, class 3
> conditions can function in a hortatory manner (i.e., don't
> love the world, though grammatically and semantically
> still a class 3 condition).

καὶ κινήσω τὴν λυχνίαν σου ἐκ τοῦ τόπου αὐτῆς, ἐὰν μὴ μετανοήσῃς.
(Rev. 2:5)

And I will remove your lampstand from its place, if you *do* not
repent.

> In a section marked by imperatives (Rev. 2:5–7), the class
> 3 condition here likely functions in a hortatory manner
> to "support the hortatory intentions of the imperatives
> in the surrounding discourse."[35] The condition presents a
> hypothetical possibility, calling for the readers to realize it.

34. Matthew has also switched the normal order of protasis-apodosis to apodosis-protasis, adding to its prominence. Luke also uses the class 3 condition for the same temptation, though he has a different order (Luke 4:7). One might contribute this to a common source (Q), rather than a desire on Matthew's part to draw attention to this temptation. However, one cannot allow a hypothesis for explaining the synoptic relationships to exercise unwarranted control in grammatical analysis. One must give priority to the text itself.

35. Mathewson, *Revelation*, 21. In Rev. 2:5–7 the class 3 condition is still a condition grammatically and semantically, which makes a projective statement in the protasis of a conditional sentence. Within the broader discourse consideration it can *function* in a hortatory way.

Exegetical Significance

As a more marked mood than the indicative, particularly in primary (independent) clauses the subjunctive mood can lend prominence to a section. It can indicate a discourse peak or serve to mark off a transition to a new section. For example, the aorist subjunctive in primary clauses with double negation (οὐ μή) functions as a strong negation of a projected statement (see οὐ μὴ τελέσητε in Gal. 5:16 above). The hortatory subjunctive plays a key role in the book of Hebrews. A cluster of subjunctives can be found in 4:11–16.

> Σπουδάσωμεν οὖν εἰσελθεῖν εἰς ἐκείνην τὴν κατάπαυσιν, ἵνα μὴ ἐν τῷ αὐτῷ τις ὑποδείγματι πέσῃ τῆς ἀπειθείας. . . . Ἔχοντες οὖν ἀρχιερέα μέγαν διεληλυθότα τοὺς οὐρανούς, Ἰησοῦν τὸν υἱὸν τοῦ θεοῦ, κρατῶμεν τῆς ὁμολογίας. . . . προσερχώμεθα οὖν μετὰ παρρησίας τῷ θρόνῳ τῆς χάριτος. (Heb. 4:11, 14, 16)
>
> Therefore, *let us strive* to enter that rest, in order that no one might fall by the same example of disobedience. . . . Therefore, having a great high priest who has passed through the heavens, Jesus, the Son of God, *let us grasp* the confession. . . . Therefore, *let us approach* with boldness the throne of grace.

The first-person plural subjunctives within a primary clause function in a commanding clause (hortatory). Along with the high-level marker οὖν, as well as expansion in the form of secondary clauses and supporting material (γάρ, vv. 12–13), the hortatory subjunctives (projective in main clauses) here function to indicate that this section is a discourse peak within Hebrews.[36]

Optative (Projection + Contingency)

The optative mood form is by far the least frequent in occurrence in the Greek of the New Testament, being found only about sixty-eight times in the entire New Testament. Roughly sixty of these instances are found in the writings of Luke-Acts and Paul.[37] A number

---

36. Westfall, *Discourse Analysis*, 136. Westfall applies SFL as a model for doing discourse analysis.
37. Mathewson and Emig, *Intermediate Greek Grammar*, 174.

of these occurrences are restricted to Paul's well-known formulaic saying μὴ γένοιτο (e.g., Rom. 6:2, 15), accounting for fifteen of the total occurrences, leaving a limited base for analysis. The most likely reason that the optative was losing ground by the time of the New Testament was, according to Porter, the awkward formal paradigm of the optative, and the fact that the overlap with the subjunctive meant that Greek speakers felt they could do with the subjunctive everything they could do with the optative, without the need to grammaticalize the additional semantic feature (+contingency) of the optative.[38]

As already noted, there is significant semantic overlap between the subjunctive and the optative, leaving the question of what the distinguishing semantic feature is. Rather than point to notions such as "wish" or "potential," Gonda explains the difference as follows: "The subjunctive . . . served him [the ancient author] to what may broadly speaking be called visualization. The optative, it would appear to me, enables the speaker to introduce elements of visualization and *contingency*, the latter being, in my opinion, the main character of this mood."[39] Likewise, Porter argues that the two primary features grammaticalized by the optative mood are projection and contingency. The optative mood, in its limited distribution across the New Testament, is used in contexts where the author wishes to portray the projected process as "slightly remoter, vaguer, less assured, or more contingent."[40] The fulfillment of the process is contingent on or "is dependent on a condition or on some event that may or may not happen."[41] Therefore, the semantic features of projection + contingency or hesitation would seem to account for the major functions of the optative in the New Testament.

The following scheme, again adapted from Porter's conceptualization of speech roles, serves to catalog the primary functions of the optative mood in the Greek New Testament. Though often used to distinguish functions of the optative (e.g., volitive, potential), it is

38. Porter, *Verbal Aspect*, 177; Porter, *Idioms*, 59.
39. Gonda, *Indo-European Moods*, 51. Italics mine.
40. Porter, *Idioms*, 59.
41. Gonda, *Indo-European Moods*, 52. "This condition or other event may be expressed, be implicit or even be vaguely or generally inherent in the situation."

doubtful that the presence or absence of the particle ἄν can be used to distinguish such functions of the optative.[42]

1. -assertive +projective -interrogative +contingent >> projective contingent statement (contingent projective clause, with optative mood form, as in volitive use)
2. -assertive +projective +interrogative
   a. +tonal +contingent >> projective contingent question (contingent projective clause, with optative mood form, as in deliberative use)
   b. +elemental +contingent >> projective contingent τ-question (contingent projective clause, with one of the question words, with optative mood form)

Projective Contingent Statements (Volitive)

-assertive +projective -interrogative +contingent >> projective contingent statement (volitive)

The optative (-assertive +projective +contingent) can make statements that function as wishes or commands. Paul's well-known use of μὴ γένοιτο belongs here as an example of a projective contingent statement. Wallace thinks that μὴ γένοιτο has become a stereotyped expression, "has lost its 'optative' flavor," and now carries the "force of abhorrence."[43] However, the fact that it may express Paul's abhorrence at an idea does not change its semantics as still making a projective, contingent statement of wish or command, dependent on the readers carrying through with what is abhorred.

μηκέτι εἰς τὸν αἰῶνα ἐκ σοῦ μηδεὶς καρπὸν φάγοι. (Mark 11:14)
May no one *eat* fruit from you again [command].

Πέτρος δὲ εἶπεν πρὸς αὐτόν· τὸ ἀργύριόν σου σὺν σοὶ *εἴη* εἰς ἀπώλειαν. (Acts 8:20)

42. Porter, *Verbal Aspect*, 174–75; Porter, *Idioms*, 60.
43. Wallace, *Greek Grammar*, 481.

And Peter said to him, "*May* your silver *be* with you unto destruction" [mild command].

ἐπιμένωμεν τῇ ἁμαρτίᾳ, ἵνα ἡ χάρις πλεονάσῃ; μὴ γένοιτο. (Rom. 6:1–2; cf. v. 15)

Should we remain in sin so that grace might increase? *May it never be!*

Αὐτὸς δὲ ὁ κύριος τῆς εἰρήνης δῴη ὑμῖν τὴν εἰρήνην διὰ παντὸς ἐν παντὶ τρόπῳ. (2 Thess. 3:16)

But *may* the Lord of peace himself *give* you peace through everything, in every way [optative expressing a wish].

Projective Contingent Questions and τ-Questions

-assertive +projective +interrogative

   a. +tonal +contingent >> projective contingent question (contingent projective clause, with optative mood form, as in deliberative use)

   b. +elemental +contingent >> projective contingent τ-question (contingent projective clause, with one of the question words, with optative mood form)

The optative is frequently used in the speech role of asking a projective, contingent question, the uncertainty in the question contingent on other factors. Some of the following examples of a projective contingent question may be indirect questions, though a case for many of them as direct questions could be made.[44]

καὶ διελογίζετο ποταπὸς εἴη ὁ ἀσπασμὸς οὗτος. (Luke 1:29)

And she [Mary] considered what manner of greeting this *might be*.

> Though this verse is usually labeled an example of an indirect question, it could be a direct question: "Mary was considering, 'What manner of greeting might this be?'"

44. Cf. Porter, *Verbal Aspect*, 176.

Προσδοκῶντος δὲ τοῦ λαοῦ καὶ διαλογιζομένων πάντων ἐν ταῖς
καρδίαις αὐτῶν περὶ τοῦ Ἰωάννου, μήποτε αὐτὸς *εἴη* ὁ χριστός.
(Luke 3:15)
And the people were waiting and were all wondering in their hearts
about John, whether he *might be* the Christ.

> Again, though sometimes analyzed as an indirect ques-
> tion, there is the possibility of this being a direct question:
> "Might he not be the Christ?"

καὶ προσκαλεσάμενος ἕνα τῶν παίδων ἐπυνθάνετο τί ἂν *εἴη* ταῦτα.
(Luke 15:26)
And he summoned one of his servants and asked, "What *might* all
these things *be*?" [projective contingent τ-question].

καί τινες ἔλεγον· τί ἂν *θέλοι* ὁ σπερμολόγος οὗτος λέγειν; (Acts
17:18)
And some said, "What *might* this babbler *wish* to say?"

> Here, the question is contingent upon whether Paul actu-
> ally speaks or not.

καὶ ἐπυνθάνετο τίς *εἴη* καὶ τί ἐστιν πεποιηκώς. (Acts 21:33)
And he inquired who *he might be* and what he had done.

> In this indirect question, notice the mixing of nonassert-
> ive, projective contingent attitude, and assertive attitude,
> perhaps suggesting more uncertainty as to who has com-
> mitted the act.

The Optative in Secondary Clauses

The optative is less frequent in secondary (dependent) clauses. It
occurs in the protasis of class 4 conditional sentences, though there
are no clear examples of a complete class 4 conditional in the New
Testament. This would be an example of a potential use of the optative, with a projective contingent statement functioning as the protasis of a conditional statement.

οὓς ἔδει ἐπὶ σοῦ παρεῖναι καὶ κατηγορεῖν <u>εἴ</u> τι ἔχοιεν πρὸς ἐμέ (Acts 24:19)

Who ought to be present before you and bring charges, <u>if</u> they *would have* anything against me

> This includes an optative in the protasis of an "incomplete" class 4 conditional sentence. There is no ἄν + optative in the apodosis, which here precedes the protasis.[45]

ἀλλ' <u>εἰ</u> καὶ *πάσχοιτε* διὰ δικαιοσύνην, μακάριοι. (1 Pet. 3:14)

But <u>if</u> also you *would suffer* for the sake of righteousness, (you are) blessed.

> This is perhaps the closest one gets to a class 4 condition in the New Testament, though there is no verb in the apodosis; the possibility for suffering is portrayed as remote.[46] See also verse 17: κρεῖττον γὰρ ἀγαθοποιοῦντας, εἰ θέλοι τὸ θέλημα τοῦ θεοῦ, πάσχειν ἢ κακοποιοῦντας (For it is better to suffer for doing good—if it might be God's will [for you to suffer]—than for doing evil).

Exegetical Significance

Due to the fact that distributionally the optative mood is the least frequently employed mood in the New Testament, its choice is probably intentional and meaningful. That is, it tends to signal prominence, particularly in primary (main) clauses. One significant usage already noted above is the negated form μὴ γένοιτο found especially in Paul's letters. As an optative used in a primary clause, it emphatically denies a statement in order to advance Paul's argument. Thus, in Romans 6:2, 15, Paul uses it twice to deny a potential objection to his argment, that grace should lead to the increase of sin. Both times this conclusion is emphatically denied with the expression μὴ γένοιτο as an absurd inference to what Paul has been arguing.

45. Mathewson and Emig, *Intermediate Greek Grammar*, 175.
46. Wallace, *Greek Grammar*, 484.

Imperative (Direction)

The mood that is perhaps the furthest away from making assertions about reality is the imperative mood, in that it only attempts to direct the action of the audience. According to Palmer, "the most common types of deontic modality are 'directives.'"[47] Very little work has been done on the semantics of the imperative mood form, particularly as it relates to the other mood forms systemically. One recent book-length analysis has been offered by Joseph Fantin.[48] Fantin suggests that "the *semantic* meaning of the imperative mood is the raw, naked imperative. It is the imperative mood at its essence. It is the meaning which is unaffected by either context or lexical contribution."[49] This bare, essential meaning of the imperative is volition or intention.[50] Fantin defines the imperative mood as follows: "The aspect of this description that is fundamental to the imperative is the notion of *volition*. Essentially, the imperative is a volitional-directive. Thus, when a communicator uses the imperative, he is presenting an intention or desire to get the recipient to 'do' something."[51] On the basis of his understanding of the semantics of the imperative mood, which he finds in every instance of the imperative in the New Testament, Fantin suggests that the *force* of the imperative depends on the context in which it occurs. Fantin follows a fairly typical categorization of imperative usages to discover whether this essential meaning is present—command, request, permission or toleration, conditional, prohibition—though he admits the difficulty of finding volition or intention in every usage. The force of the imperative, however, can be reduced, according to Fantin, through various weakening strategies: an introductory word (e.g., "I exhort you . . ."), third-person imperative, and the use of honor terms with the imperative. Fantin does come close to a philosophical and essentialist definition of the imperative that seems to overemphasize the essential *inherent*

47. Palmer, *Mood and Modality*, 70.
48. Fantin, *Greek Imperative Mood*. See also his shorter treatment, "May the *Force* Be with You."
49. Fantin, *Greek Imperative Mood*, 122. Italics his.
50. Fantin, *Greek Imperative Mood*, 133–34. Here Fantin is heavily dependent on the work of Wallace (*Greek Grammar*, 485).
51. Fantin, "May the *Force* Be with You," 186. Italics his.

meaning an imperative has apart from its linguistic context. There is no inherent meaning attached to lexical or grammatical items, and the concept of a noncontextual meaning is problematic. He also relies on typical labels that ostensibly capture the various functions of the imperative without ever questioning their validity or the criteria (usually not linguistic) for determining them. Furthermore, he is not clear on what the relationship is between the *semantics* of the imperative and its *force*, particularly if the latter can be weakened by different strategies. Fantin's work also seems to treat the imperative mood in isolation and shows limited interest in its clear relationship to the other mood forms.

In a helpful article on the semantics of the imperative mood in New Testament Greek, and partly in interaction with Fantin, James Dvorak chooses SFL as a useful way of understanding the semantics of the imperative mood, or what he calls the "ethnographic-descriptive paradigm" approach to meaning. Under this model, Dvorak understands the imperative mood within the context of culture and context of situation. "The reason that linguistic forms evoke a field of meaning is because the use of those signs has become associated with particular situational contextual frames within a culture. When those contexts of situation recur, they at once activate and constrain (but do not dictate) certain kinds of meaning that are appropriate to the context, which in turn activates and constrains lexicogrammatical options, which may be selected by the language user to make meaning in that context of situation in a sensible way."[52] Following Porter, Dvorak proposes that the imperative mood grammaticalizes the semantic feature of *direction*. More specifically, he says, "In cultural and situational contexts where it is appropriate, the imperative mood form grammaticalizes the language user's selection of directive attitude, which is the typical or congruent selection from the linguistic system when a language user proposes to direct someone's behavior, thoughts, beliefs, and/or feelings."[53] In this way, Dvorak develops a unified semantic approach based on the cultural context and context of situation and expressed lexicogrammatically in the verbal endings.

52. Dvorak, "'Evidence That Commands a Verdict,'" 213–14.
53. Dvorak, "'Evidence That Commands a Verdict,'" 215.

Though these studies differ widely in their linguistic approaches and the results they obtain, there is at least broad agreement that the semantic feature of direction or volition is the main feature communicated by the selection of the imperative mood form.[54] Therefore, within a given context of situation that activates directive as a semantic option, the author can make the grammatical selection of the imperative mood form to realize this meaning potential. As one of the nonassertive moods, then, the imperative mood is directive in meaning. Although the imperative shares with the subjunctive and optative the feature of -assertion, the difference between the two can be explained: "The subjunctive/optative grammaticalizes a projected visualization by the speaker, and the imperative grammaticalizes simply the speaker's direction of the audience toward a process."[55] As already noted, the subjunctive mood in the second person is used for aorist prohibitions, and the first-person subjunctive can be used for commands (so-called hortatory subjunctive), showing overlap in function between the two moods. Furthermore, the future can also be used to express a command (see below), as well as the optative mood form. It is important to remember that these mood forms (and the future) all retain their semantic force despite overlap in speech roles: subjunctive = projection; optative = projection and contingency; imperative = direction; future = expectation (see below). As Porter notes, "These semantic features are realized regardless of the uses to which they may be put within a given discourse, however these may be described, categorized, or differentiated."[56] The imperative mood grammaticalizes the semantic feature of direction in the various discourse contexts in which it occurs.[57] The choice of the imperative can be conceptualized as follows:

-assertive +directive >> command (imperative mood form)

54. It would be incorrect to say that the imperative refers to future time. In one sense it is true that if the process directed by the imperative mood is actualized it would take place sometime after the issuing of the imperative. However, the readers may or may not choose to carry out the directive, making a reference to future time in conjunction with the imperative mood problematic.

55. Porter, "Aspect and Imperatives," 144.

56. Porter, "Aspect and Imperatives," 163.

57. Von Siebenthal, *Ancient Greek Grammar*, 359: the imperative expresses "directives."

The imperative mood form realizes the speech role of "demanding goods and services."

The imperative form can be utilized in both second- and third-person forms, for both general and specific commands. Both forms can also be negated with μή to form a prohibition. As already observed, the second-person prohibition of the aorist is expressed with the aorist subjunctive with μή (see above under "Projective Statements").

Commands

καὶ ἐπετίμησεν αὐτῷ ὁ Ἰησοῦς λέγων· *φιμώθητι* καὶ *ἔξελθε* ἀπ᾽ αὐτοῦ. (Luke 4:35)

And Jesus rebuked him, saying, "*Be silent* and *come out* of him."

πάντα εἰς δόξαν θεοῦ *ποιεῖτε*. (1 Cor. 10:31)

Do all things for the glory of God.

Γυνὴ ἐν ἡσυχίᾳ *μανθανέτω* ἐν πάσῃ ὑποταγῇ. (1 Tim. 2:11)

A woman *should learn* in silence in all submission.

Γίνεσθε δὲ ποιηταὶ λόγου καὶ μὴ μόνον ἀκροαταί. (James 1:22)

But *become* doers of the word and not hearers only.

Prohibitions

Μὴ *κρίνετε*, ἵνα μὴ κριθῆτε. (Matt. 7:1)

Do not *judge*, in order that you might not be judged.

Μὴ οὖν *βασιλευέτω* ἡ ἁμαρτία ἐν τῷ θνητῷ ὑμῶν σώματι. (Rom. 6:12)

Therefore, sin *should* not *reign* in your mortal bodies.

καὶ εἷς ἐκ τῶν πρεσβυτέρων λέγει μοι· μὴ *κλαῖε*. (Rev. 5:5)

And one of the elders said to me, "*Do* not *weep*" [prohibits an action already going on].

Third-Person Imperatives

Although a common way of translating third-person imperatives is with the gloss "let . . . ," it is important to note that third-person imperatives are just as directive as the second person.[58] They are not permissive; that is, they are not commands for someone to allow or let someone else do something. For this reason the translation gloss "should" is used above.[59] However, at times the third-person imperative may have the effect of indirectly commanding someone to do something or focus on the grammatical subject as something the readers are to follow.

ὁ ἥλιος μὴ ἐπιδυέτω ἐπὶ [τῷ] παροργισμῷ ὑμῶν. (Eph. 4:26)

The sun *should not set* upon your anger.

> Here the third person may be used to focus on an important virtue that Paul wants believers to follow. Obviously, Paul has no say whether the sun sets or not, but he issues a third-person command that can only be carried out by his readers. So the third-person imperative here allows Paul to focus on the grammatical subject "sun" in order to ultimately direct his readers toward what to avoid.

ἔστω δὲ πᾶς ἄνθρωπος ταχὺς εἰς τὸ ἀκοῦσαι, βραδὺς εἰς τὸ λαλῆσαι, βραδὺς εἰς ὀργήν. (James 1:19)

But every person *should be* quick to hear, slow to speak, and slow to anger.

> The third-person imperative ἔστω with the subject πᾶς ἄνθρωπος may function as an indirect command for the readers.

Requests

Though further labels such as "entreaty," "request," or "permission" may capture the pragmatic force of the imperative in certain

58. "Greek's 3d person imperative is, however, every bit as direct as its 2d person imperative" (G. Long, *Grammatical Concepts*, 80).
59. Cf. Mathewson and Emig, *Intermediate Greek Grammar*, 176–77; von Siebenthal, *Ancient Greek Grammar*, 359.

contexts, it is important to realize that the semantic notion of direction is still present in these usages. According to Dvorak, "directive may be interpreted as an entreaty or petition. Nevertheless, it is still a directive."[60] Such labels rely on an unprincipled appeal to inconsistent criteria and overlook the fact that the author's choice of the imperative mood as part of the mood system is the result of a context of situation that activates a certain meaning, which in turn activates a lexicogrammatical expression (the imperative mood). Such labels often fail to consider the relationship between *usage* and the *semantics* of the imperative form. Thus, any additional features are not part of the semantics of the imperative mood and often depend on a mixture of discourse and extralinguistic features.

κύριε, βοήθει μοι. (Matt. 15:25)
Lord, *help* me.

> This is usually considered an entreaty or request, though the semantics of "give a directive" are still present. The issue of how this would have been understood in the social context in which it was uttered raises many complex issues.

ἔρχου κύριε Ἰησοῦ. (Rev. 22:20)
Come, Lord Jesus.

> The imperative ἔρχου can be seen as having the force of a request, but it is still directive.

Imperative and Verbal Aspect

One important and much-discussed issue surrounding imperative forms is their usage with verbal aspect.[61] The imperative mood is virtually restricted to the aorist/present opposition. Without chronicling the detailed history, much of the discussion has been informed by

---

60. Dvorak, "'Evidence That Commands a Verdict,'" 217.
61. Mathewson, "Verbal Aspect in Imperatival Constructions"; Porter, "Aspect and Imperatives."

Aktionsart (kind of action) approaches to the imperative mood and the aorist and present tense forms, so that a number of assumed "rules" have crystallized around the use of the imperative mood (and subjunctive with aorist prohibitions). For example, based on *Aktionsart* approaches it is often concluded that aorist imperative = specific command, present imperative = general command; or aorist imperative = beginning action, present imperative = continuing action. For prohibitions, present imperative with μή = command to cease an action taking place ("Stop . . ."); aorist subjunctive with μή = command not to begin an action ("Don't start . . ."). Despite protests very early on,[62] this view still largely persists in grammars and other treatments of the imperative mood.[63]

However, there are at least two problems with this approach. First, it is inconsistent with verbal aspect, which like its use in other moods sees the verbal morphology as grammaticalizing the author's subjective conception of the process, not the objective nature of the action itself. Instead, the difference is one of verbal aspect.[64] Differing kinds of actions can be directed using the present or aorist forms, depending on the author's conception of the process. Second, there are too many examples that do not conform to these so-called rules of usage. For example, the specific/general distinction in relationship to aorist/present contrast is a broad observable pattern, but with plenty of exceptions. This is explicable if the tense forms grammaticalize verbal aspect rather than kind of action. Consequently, the different forms used for directing a process can better be understood along the lines of the semantics of the imperative (or subjunctive) forms and the semantics of verbal aspect:

> Present imperative—direction toward a process viewed as in progress

62. Cf. Donovan, "Sonnenschein's Greek Grammar"; Louw, "On Greek Prohibitions."

63. See Fanning, *Verbal Aspect in New Testament Greek*, 325–79; Wallace, *Greek Grammar*, 718–22; Campbell, *Verbal Aspect in Non-Indicative Verbs*, 79–100.

64. Cf. Porter, *Verbal Aspect*, 335–63; Mathewson, "Verbal Aspect in Imperatival Constructions"; McKay, "Aspect in Imperatival Constructions"; Huffman, *Verbal Aspect Theory*; Porter, "Aspect and Imperatives."

Aorist imperative—direction toward a process viewed as a complete whole

Present prohibition (present imperative with μή)—direction toward denial of a process viewed as in progress

Aorist prohibition (second person aorist subjunctive with μή; third person aorist imperative with μή)—direction toward / projection of denial of a process viewed as a complete whole

In each of these cases, whether the action is general or specific, already begun or not, depends on discourse usage. Any of these constructions can be used of action that is specific or general, or that has not yet begun or is *already* taking place. Such notions depend on broader (usually extralinguistic) contextual features and are not grammaticalized in the imperative (subjunctive) forms themselves.

Τεκνία, φυλάξατε ἑαυτὰ ἀπὸ τῶν εἰδώλων. (1 John 5:21)

Children, *guard* yourselves from idols.

> First John ends with an imperative in the aorist tense form, but one which is clearly general in nature (not a specific "one-off" injunction).[65]

ὁ δὲ εἶπεν· φέρετέ μοι ὧδε αὐτούς. (Matt. 14:18)

And he [Jesus] said [to them], "*Bring* them here to me."

> Here, a present imperative is used of a specific command, for an action that has apparently not yet begun.

μὴ θαυμάσῃς ὅτι εἶπόν σοι· δεῖ ὑμᾶς γεννηθῆναι ἄνωθεν. (John 3:7)

Do not marvel that I told you it is necessary for you all to be born again.

> The aorist subjunctive prohibition is used to interrupt action already taking place, as the previous context makes clear in verses 3–6.

---

65. Whether the readers are already involved in the process or not is not clear from the context, so "start . . ." is not required or warranted.

εἴ τις ἀδελφὸς γυναῖκα ἔχει ἄπιστον καὶ αὕτη συνευδοκεῖ οἰκεῖν μετ᾽ αὐτοῦ, μὴ ἀφιέτω αὐτήν. (1 Cor. 7:12)

If a certain brother has an unbelieving wife, and she consents to live with him, he *should not divorce* her.

> The notion "stop divorcing" does not work in this instance, since μὴ ἀφιέτω is a general prohibition, apparently aimed at preventing anyone (τις ἀδελφὸς) from divorcing.

κράτει ὃ ἔχεις, ἵνα μηδεὶς λάβῃ τὸν στέφανόν σου. (Rev. 3:11)

Grasp what you have, in order that no one might take your crown.

> The present imperative κράτει might be in this context a call to continue to hang on to something they are already hanging on to, since the surrounding context makes clear they have kept the word and have endured (vv. 8, 10).

Exegetical Significance

The imperative mood tends to lend prominence to the discourse, against assertions made in the background indicative mood. "There is a graded increase in prominence as we move away from fact toward volition and action."[66] For example, one cannot fail to notice the shift in mood from indicative to predominantly imperative mood forms in Ephesians 1–3 and 4–6. The indicative mood in chapters 1–3 lays down assertive declarative statements regarding the believers' position in Christ. The shift to the imperative mood, then, in chapters 4–6 foregrounds through the imperative mood the directives that highlight the appropriate (ethical) response of the readers based on the assertions made in chapters 1–3.

Frequently the aspect of the imperative is significant, with the aorist normally being the unmarked form, and the present being the more marked form of the aorist/present opposition. In Romans 6:12–15 the reader encounters an interplay between aorist and present imperative forms. The positive command is in the aorist imperative (v. 13: παραστήσατε), whereas the contrasting prohibitions are present

---

66. Callow, "Patterns of Thematic Development," 197.

imperatives (with μή) (vv. 12–13: μὴ βασιλευέτω, μηδὲ παριστάνετε).
Rather than evoking the artificial contrast between "stop doing" and
"start doing," the present tense likely serves to draw attention to and
resume the main theme of verses 1–2: freedom from sin's reign. The
present prohibitions continue the theme of being dead to sin and
freedom from its reign and highlight what is to be avoided in light
of this. The aorist, then, simply recalls and summarizes the positive
corollary to this.[67]

The Future Form

Though it is not technically part of the mood system in Greek,
something must be said briefly about the future form and how it
might fit into the discussion of mood. Most grammarians recognize
the difficulty in categorizing the future tense form. Formally and
semantically it exhibits similarities with the subjunctive mood. Does
it belong with the other aspects as part of the aspectual system of
Greek? Is it a true temporal (tense) form? Is it a mood? McKay sees it
as "something of an anomaly in the ancient Greek verb system" but
treats it as a fourth aspect expressing intention.[68] Porter concludes
that it is "aspectually vague," participating in features of both the
aspectual and the mood system, without belonging fully to either.[69]
Unlike the mood forms, the future does not develop morphologically across the other aspects. Without settling the debate here of
how precisely we categorize the future form grammatically, if it is
aspectually vague, at the very least the formal and semantic similarities with the subjunctive warrant treating it along with the other
moods, even if it is not fully a mood and could still also be treated
along with the other aspectual forms. Porter argues that the future
form semantically encodes the notion of *expectation*.[70] This would
still fit with grammarians who see the future form as referring to future time: it indicates action that the author expects is going to take

---

67. Mathewson, "Verbal Aspect in Imperatival Constructions," 25–30; Mathewson and Emig, *Intermediate Greek Grammar*, 182.
68. McKay, *New Syntax*, 34.
69. Porter, *Verbal Aspect*, chap. 9.
70. Porter, *Idioms*, 44; see also Mathewson and Emig, *Intermediate Greek Grammar*, 137.

place. Therefore it implicates future time, though there are instances of the future used outside of reference to future time (see χρηματίσει in Rom. 7:3).[71] Its overlap in functions with the subjunctive mood (deliberative, command), and its usage in contexts where one might expect the subjunctive (e.g., in ἵνα clauses; cf. Rev. 3:9: ἵνα ἥξουσιν καὶ προσκυνήσουσιν [in order that they *will come* and *will worship*]),[72] suggests its semantic similarity with that mood. However, in contexts where one expects to find the subjunctive form but finds the future, the future will be the more semantically weighty form with its feature of expectation. Perhaps it can be seen as having elements of both the assertive and nonassertive moods. There is probably much more to say about the future in relationship to the Greek verbal system, but if the future form encodes the feature of expectation, one way that the future form could be seen in relationship to the Greek mood system might be as follows:

Mood	Meaning
Indicative	Assertion
Future	Expectation of fulfillment
Subjunctive	Projection (no expectation of fulfillment)
Optative	Projection (contingent expectation of fulfillment)
Imperative	Direction

Placing the future form between the indicative and the other nonindicative moods, as I have done here, shows (1) its similarities with both the indicative mood, since it morphologically resembles present indicative forms, and the nonindicative moods, as it stands sort of in between the two; and (2) that, based on similarities with the nonassertive moods, it makes a stronger statement regarding expectation of fulfillment than the other nonassertive moods. The future tense would present a process as an assertion that the author, by choice of the future form, expects to be realized or fulfilled, which shares features with projection. Hence, it is more semantically forceful than the subjunctive, which only projects a process but indicates

71. See Porter, *Verbal Aspect*, 421–24, for other examples.
72. Mathewson, *Revelation*, 48.

no expectation of fulfillment. This analysis accounts for a number of important functions of the future. The only functions to be considered below will be those that demonstrate its similarity with the other nonassertive moods.

Prospective

This is the usage that most grammarians would identify as central to the semantics and function of the future tense form. In certain contextual environments the future form, indicating expectation or intention, implicates future time reference in terms of a prediction of events expected to take place. The notion of *expectation* in the future is not dissimilar to *projection*, found in the subjunctive and optative moods.

οὕτως *ἐλεύσεται* ὃν τρόπον ἐθεάσασθε αὐτὸν πορευόμενον εἰς τὸν οὐρανόν. (Acts 1:11)
So he [Jesus] *will come* in the same manner you saw him going into heaven.

τὸ θηρίον τὸ ἀναβαῖνον ἐκ τῆς ἀβύσσου *ποιήσει* μετ᾽ αὐτῶν πόλεμον καὶ *νικήσει* αὐτοὺς καὶ *ἀποκτενεῖ* αὐτούς. (Rev. 11:7)
The beast that comes up out of the abyss *will make* war with them and *will overcome* them and *will kill* them.

Deliberative or Intention

The future can also, similar to the other nonassertive moods, in certain contexts express deliberation or intention on the part of the agent.

εἶπέν τις πρὸς αὐτόν· *ἀκολουθήσω* σοι ὅπου ἐὰν ἀπέρχῃ. (Luke 9:57)
A certain one said to him, "I *intend to follow* you wherever you go."

πῶς *γνωσθήσεται* τὸ αὐλούμενον ἢ τὸ κιθαριζόμενον; . . . πῶς *γνωσθήσεται* τὸ λαλούμενον; (1 Cor. 14:7, 9)
How *will* anyone *know* what is being played on the flute or on the harp? . . . How *will* anyone *know* what is being said?

Command

Overlapping with the imperative mood and subjunctive mood, the future form can function to express a command or prohibition. Compared to the imperative and subjunctive, the future form is semantically more forceful, grammaticalizing expectation toward the process.

καὶ καλέσεις τὸ ὄνομα αὐτοῦ Ἰησοῦν. (Matt. 1:21)
And you *shall call* his name Jesus [command].

γέγραπται ὅτι οὐκ ἐπ᾽ ἄρτῳ μόνῳ ζήσεται ὁ ἄνθρωπος. (Luke 4:4)
It is written that a person *shall not live* by bread alone [prohibition].

Conclusion

The mood system in Greek consists of a system of formal and semantic choices from assertive and nonassertive moods. The assertive mood is represented by the indicative mood, while the nonassertive choice is represented by further nuanced attitudinal choices: subjunctive, optative, and imperative. Though perhaps not fully aspectual or modal, the future can at least be seen in relationship to the other moods as grammaticalizing the semantic feature of expectation. The moods in Greek contribute to the interpersonal function of the language, where the clause functions as an interactive event between author and readers.[73] Mood plays a significant role in indicating how the author of a biblical text interacts with his readers in terms of the speech roles language can be used to perform.[74] For example, the predominance of the indicative mood in a text, or section of text, can indicate the author's desire to convey information to the readers. In narrative it is used to express events that the author believes to have taken place. The predominance of the imperative mood (or the subjunctive functioning in a hortatory manner or as a prohibition) indicates the author's desire to direct the actions of the readers by issuing commands and prohibitions that the biblical author expects

73. Halliday, *Functional Grammar*, 68.
74. Reed, *Discourse Analysis of Philippians*, 347.

his readers to follow (since presumably he is in a position to offer such directives). More projective moods can indicate the author's desire to be less direct or make less-certain statements by projecting possible or contingent actions. Questions will indicate the author's intention to demand information or a response from the readers. One pattern that can often be discerned in Paul's letters is the use of the assertive mood to make statements, followed by commands and injunctions in the imperative mood. The assertions in the indicative mood provide the basis for the directives in the imperative mood forms (cf. Eph. 1–3; 4–6). Noticing such patterns of mood usage over larger stretches of discourse while analyzing the interpersonal function of a text can be more important than merely labeling and classifying individual instances of mood forms in the Greek New Testament, as is the disposition of most Greek grammars.

6

Infinitives and Participles

Though not technically part of the mood system in Greek, since they do not grammaticalize mood in terms of assertiveness or nonassertiveness, infinitives and participles will be treated here also. The semantic notions communicated by the infinitive and participle, presupposing rather than asserting the author's commitment to the truth of a proposition (participle) or not (infinitive),[1] is not completely dissimilar to the assertive and nonassertive notions communicated in the mood forms. However, in another sense they can still be viewed like mood in terms of the author's commitment to the truth or reality of the action of the verb, though not in terms of either assertion or nonassertion, but in terms of what they presuppose (see below). Both the infinitive and participle are similar in that they do not grammaticalize and so are not limited by one or both features of person (infinitive and participle) and number (infinitive). That is, they are considered nonfinite verbal forms within the overall verbal system. The infinitive and participle are often regarded by grammars as hybrid forms, since they exhibit features of both the verb and the noun or adjective.[2] Therefore, as a verbal form infinitives grammaticalize aspect and voice while also showing affinities to the noun syntactically (e.g., they can take an article, they

1. See Porter, *Verbal Aspect*, 390–91.
2. Cf. Porter, *Idioms*, 181, 194; Wallace, *Greek Grammar*, 588–89, 613–17; Mathewson and Emig, *Intermediate Greek Grammar*, 192, 205; von Siebenthal, *Ancient Greek Grammar*, 362, 382.

can fill the noun slot in a clause). Likewise, the participle exhibits aspect and voice, but like a substantive or adjective, also exhibits case and gender. The participle also manifests several syntactical functions similar to the Greek adjective (thus its common designation by some grammars as a "verbal adjective"). Unlike the infinitive, the participle also communicates number (singular and plural).

What, then, is the primary semantic distinction between the Greek infinitive and participle? What semantic features are grammaticalized in the two forms? As already noted, at one level the participle could be seen as a verbal adjective, and the infinitive as a verbal noun. Yet it is possible to be more specific. Von Siebenthal concludes that "the main function of the Ancient Greek participle is to present the 'action' of the verb as the property (either actual or potential) of an entity."[3] Thus, participles have case, gender, and number in addition to aspect and voice, which they presumably derive from the entity of which they are the property. By contrast, the function of the Greek infinitive is simply to "refer to the 'action' of the verb."[4] Porter treats infinitives and participles in terms of the notions that they grammaticalize, which can then be semantically differentiated.[5] According to Porter, the participle grammaticalizes the feature of +factive presupposition. That is, the participle expresses the presupposition (not the assertion) that the author is committed to the truth or reality of the action of the verb. Drawing on Palmer's treatment of modality, the participle presupposes the author's commitment to the truth of a proposition.[6] With participles, the action is "known to, presupposed by, both the speaker and the addressee. . . . What is at issue is that nothing is being asserted, that there is no information value, because both the speaker and the hearer accept the proposition."[7] Hence, it is only presupposed. By contrast, the infinitive makes no such presupposition. Therefore, it does not communicate factive presupposition

---

3. Von Siebenthal, *Ancient Greek Grammar*, 382.
4. Von Siebenthal, *Ancient Greek Grammar*, 362.
5. Porter, *Verbal Aspect*, 391. Cf. Porter, "Prominence," 64.
6. Porter, *Verbal Aspect*, 391.
7. Palmer, *Mood and Modality*, 4. Though Palmer is not at this point discussing participle forms.

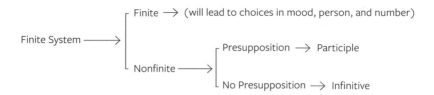

Figure 6.1

(-factive presupposition) but only refers to the action.[8] That is, the infinitive merely states the verbal idea.

Therefore, it seems best to understand the participle and infinitive along these lines. The participle (unlike the indicative mood) does not make an assertion about reality but grammaticalizes the author's intent to *presuppose the truth or reality of the action*, accepting the proposition. By contrast, the infinitive makes no such presupposition but merely *refers to the action of the verb* and presupposes or states nothing about it. This probably accounts for the use of the two forms primarily in secondary and embedded clauses, in modifying roles. Like other features within the Greek verb, the participle and infinitive represent distinct semantic choices within the finite system.

This unified semantic feature of each form serves to circumscribe and account for the various functions of the infinitive and participle in the Greek New Testament. The following discussion will proceed with the above description of the semantics of the infinitive and participle forms. The ensuing treatment of infinitives and participles will, in light of the main semantic contribution of the two forms, consider the primary functions of each form. These will be illustrated by several examples from the Greek New Testament. The intent is to be not exhaustive but illustrative.

Infinitives

As noted above, the Greek infinitive can be seen as possessing features of both the verb and the noun (often called a "verbal noun").

8. Porter, *Verbal Aspect*, 391.

However, semantically the choice of the infinitive from the choice of nonfinite in the Greek verbal system indicates no presupposition regarding the reality or truth of the action in the verbal process (see fig. 6.1). Rather, the infinitive merely refers to the action of the verbal idea. The infinitive as a verb form expresses aspect and voice but is not limited by person and number. It can also take an object, subject, and adjuncts. The infinitive can take an article, suggesting its possible functions as a substantive, and can occur in the same syntactical environments that nouns do.[9]

Excursus: The "Subject" of the Infinitive

As already noted, the infinitive is not limited by person and number, so that the agent of the action in active voice constructions, or the medium of the action in middle/passive voice constructions, is not grammaticalized in the verbal ending. Quite often, the subject (agent or medium) of the action expressed by the infinitive will be identical to that of the main verb.

Μὴ νομίσητε ὅτι ἦλθον *καταλῦσαι* τὸν νόμον ἢ τοὺς προφήτας. (Matt. 5:17)

Do not think that I have come *to destroy* the law and the prophets.

> The subject of the infinitive in this instance is the same as the verb that it modifies, ἦλθον, referring to Jesus. However, the subject of the infinitive can also be expressed grammatically with a substantive in the accusative case.

μετανοήσατε οὖν καὶ ἐπιστρέψατε εἰς τὸ *ἐξαλειφθῆναι* ὑμῶν <u>τὰς ἁμαρτίας</u>. (Acts 3:19)

Therefore, repent and turn so that your <u>sins</u> *might be erased*.

> The accusative substantive τὰς ἁμαρτίας functions as the subject and medium of the passive voice infinitive ἐξαλειφθῆναι.

9. See von Siebenthal (*Ancient Greek Grammar*, 362) for further ways the infinitive resembles verbs and nouns.

ἵνα καταργηθῇ τὸ σῶμα τῆς ἁμαρτίας, τοῦ μηκέτι δουλεύειν ἡμᾶς τῇ ἁμαρτίᾳ (Rom. 6:6)

In order that the body of sin might be destroyed, in order that <u>we</u> *might* no longer *serve* sin

> The accusative pronoun ἡμᾶς functions as the subject and agent of the active voice infinitive δουλεύειν.

This phenomenon of the accusative "subject" with infinitives is often explained as the substantive functioning as an accusative of respect. While this may indeed be the case, it is still important to recognize that the accusative case is functioning in these examples (and others) as the subject (either agent or medium) of the infinitive.[10] Thus, I will simply refer to these accusatives as subjects of the infinitive. This raises the further issue of an infinitive with two accusative nouns, one functioning as the subject and the other as the direct object (or medium). Given that both are in the accusative case, identification can be problematic. A guideline that holds in many instances is that the subject will precede the direct object.[11]

διὰ τὸ ἔχειν <u>με</u> ἐν τῇ καρδίᾳ <u>ὑμᾶς</u> (Phil. 1:7)

Because <u>I</u> *have* <u>you</u> in (my) heart [or, Because <u>you</u> *have* <u>me</u> in (your) heart]

> This construction is ambiguous with regard to the function of the two accusative pronouns. The question is which one functions as the subject and which one the direct object of the infinitive ἔχειν. However, the word order suggests that με should be understood as the subject, and ὑμᾶς as the direct object.[12] Thus, the first translation above is probably correct: "Because I have you in (my) heart."

10. Porter, *Idioms*, 202; Wallace, *Greek Grammar*, 192; Mathewson and Emig, *Intermediate Greek Grammar*, 193–94; von Siebenthal, *Ancient Greek Grammar*, 364–65.

11. Porter, *Idioms*, 203. Cf. Reed, "Infinitive with Two Accusative Substantives." For a dissenting view to this approach, see Wallace, *Greek Grammar*, 193–94. See his critique of Reed on p. 164n62.

12. Most recently, this view is adopted by Novakovic, *Philippians*, 9–10.

The above summary forms the basis for the following discussion of the major functions of the infinitive in the Greek New Testament. Though there may be other ways of organizing the functions of the infinitive, the way of examining the infinitive functions here proceeds according to the possible slots they can fill in a clause structure: substantive slot, noun/adjective modifier, adverbial adjunct slot, articular infinitive with a preposition, or predicate slot.

Substantive Slot

An infinitive form can fill the syntactical slot of a substantive, functioning in a variety of ways similar to a noun. The fact that the infinitive merely states the verbal idea and does not presuppose the reality of the action of the verbal process makes it possible for it to function in a variety of syntactical contexts and substitute for the use of the noun in a clause, usually as subject or direct object. It is important to realize that the infinitive in these contexts semantically is still an infinitive and communicates the verbal notions of aspect and voice, while merely stating the verbal idea. The following functions can be discerned.

Subject

The infinitive can fill the syntactical slot of the subject of a verb in a clause. This use of the infinitive often occurs with impersonal-type verbs (e.g., ἔξεστιν).[13] The use of the infinitive with δεῖ could also be included here (see below under "Catenative Constructions").[14]

οἱ μαθηταί σου ποιοῦσιν ὃ οὐκ ἔξεστιν *ποιεῖν* ἐν σαββάτῳ. (Matt. 12:2)

Your disciples are doing what it is not right *to do* on the Sabbath [with the impersonal verb ἔξεστιν].

Ἐμοὶ γὰρ τὸ *ζῆν* Χριστὸς καὶ τὸ *ἀποθανεῖν* κέρδος. (Phil. 1:21; cf. v. 24: τὸ ἐπιμένειν)

For to me *to live* is Christ and *to die* is gain.

---

13. Porter, *Idioms*, 195; von Siebenthal, *Ancient Greek Grammar*, 366.
14. Mathewson and Emig, *Intermediate Greek Grammar*, 195.

> This is perhaps the "classic" example of the infinitive filling the subject slot of a verbless clause. In both instances the infinitive is articular, further indicating its use as a substantive.

μετὰ ταῦτα δεῖ *λυθῆναι* αὐτὸν μικρὸν χρόνον. (Rev. 20:3)
After these things it is necessary for him *to be loosed* for a short while.

> The passive infinitive functions as the subject of δεῖ, also taking a "subject" in the accusative (αὐτὸν).

Object

An infinitive can also serve to fill the syntactical slot of direct object of a clause. A number of different types of constructions may be considered here.

Verbal Complement

In this usage, the infinitive seems syntactically to function to complete the idea of the verb.

ἄφετε τὰ παιδία *ἔρχεσθαι* πρός με. (Mark 10:14)
Permit the children *to come* to me.

νυνὶ δὲ καὶ *τὸ ποιῆσαι* ἐπιτελέσατε. (2 Cor. 8:11)
But now also finish *doing* (it).

> The articular infinitive τὸ ποιῆσαι is the complement of the imperative ἐπιτελέσατε.[15]

Catenative Constructions

This use of the infinitive could be considered as a subset of the usage of the infinitive as the object of verbs. The most common verbs used in these constructions are δεῖ, δύναμαι, θέλω, or μέλλω. That is, the infinitive can be seen as functioning to fill the syntactical slot

15. Mathewson and Emig, *Intermediate Greek Grammar*, 196.

of direct object with these verbs. On the other hand, this function of the infinitive may also warrant its own treatment since this function occurs with specific types of verbs (often called a "complementary infinitive"). Together the verb and the infinitive occupy the same syntactical slot and function to communicate the verbal idea in the clausal unit.

τοῦτο τὸ γένος ἐν οὐδενὶ δύναται ἐξελθεῖν εἰ μὴ ἐν προσευχῇ. (Mark 9:29)

This kind is not able *to come out* except with prayer.

ἔδει πληρωθῆναι τὴν γραφὴν ἣν προεῖπεν τὸ πνεῦμα τὸ ἅγιον. (Acts 1:16)

It was necessary for the writings *to be fulfilled* that the Holy Spirit spoke beforehand.

οὐ θέλω δὲ ὑμᾶς ἀγνοεῖν, ἀδελφοί. (Rom. 1:13)

I do not want you *to be ignorant*, brothers and sisters.

ἰδοὺ μέλλει βάλλειν ὁ διάβολος ἐξ ὑμῶν εἰς φυλακὴν ἵνα πειρασθῆτε. (Rev. 2:10)

Look, the devil is about *to throw* some of you into prison in order that you might be tested.

Indirect Discourse

After verbs whose lexical meaning conveys perception the infinitive can function to indicate the object or content of the verbal process. "An infinitive can be used as an object of a verb of perception (speaking, thinking, and the like) to convey indirect speech."[16] The meaning of the infinitive as simply stating the verbal idea without presupposing anything lends itself to this usage.

τίνα λέγουσιν οἱ ἄνθρωποι εἶναι τὸν υἱὸν τοῦ ἀνθρώπου; (Matt. 16:13)

Who do people say the son of man *is*?

16. Porter, *Idioms*, 197.

οὕτως καὶ ὑμεῖς λογίζεσθε ἑαυτοὺς *εἶναι* νεκροὺς μὲν τῇ ἁμαρτίᾳ ζῶντας δὲ τῷ θεῷ ἐν Χριστῷ Ἰησοῦ. (Rom. 6:11)

You also consider yourselves *to be* dead to sin, on the one hand, but living to God in Christ Jesus.

τῶν λεγόντων ἑαυτοὺς Ἰουδαίους *εἶναι* (Rev. 3:9)

Those who say that they *are* Jews

Noun/Adjective Modifier

The infinitive can be used to modify a noun or adjective element in a clause, or a larger syntactical unit, further specifying the modified element. This is often labeled by grammarians as the appositional or epexegetical use of the infinitive. This function could be included with the discussion of the adverbial adjunct below, since they both express the same function of modifying another element in the clause, rather than functioning as an element of the clause. However, I have separated them according to whether they modify a substantive element or larger syntactical unit, or whether they modify a verbal element.

οὐκέτι εἰμὶ ἄξιος *κληθῆναι* υἱός σου. (Luke 15:19)

I am not worthy *to be called* your son.

> The infinitive κληθῆναι modifies the adjective ἄξιος.

θρησκεία καθαρὰ καὶ ἀμίαντος παρὰ τῷ θεῷ καὶ πατρὶ αὕτη ἐστίν, *ἐπισκέπτεσθαι* ὀρφανοὺς καὶ χήρας ἐν τῇ θλίψει αὐτῶν, ἄσπιλον ἑαυτὸν *τηρεῖν* ἀπὸ τοῦ κόσμου. (James 1:27)

Pure and undefiled religion before (our) God and Father is this: *to visit* orphans and widows in their distress, *to keep* yourself unstained from the world.

> The two infinitives are in apposition to and modify the demonstrative pronoun αὕτη.

Καὶ ἐδόθη αὐτῷ στόμα λαλοῦν μεγάλα καὶ βλασφημίας καὶ ἐδόθη αὐτῷ ἐξουσία *ποιῆσαι* μῆνας τεσσεράκοντα [καὶ] δύο. (Rev. 13:5)

And he [the beast] was given a mouth *to speak* great and blasphemous things, and he was given authority *to act* for forty-two months.

> Both infinitives modify substantives in these clauses.

Adverbial Adjunct Slot

Like the use of the infinitive to modify nouns, a very frequent function of the infinitive is to fill the syntactical slot of an adverbial adjunct and modify a verbal form in a sentence.

The infinitive, with or without the article (τοῦ), can fill the slot of an adverbial adjunct in a clause, expressing purpose or result. Sometimes distinguishing the two semantic notions of purpose and result is difficult.

εἴδομεν γὰρ αὐτοῦ τὸν ἀστέρα ἐν τῇ ἀνατολῇ καὶ ἤλθομεν *προσκυνῆσαι* αὐτῷ. (Matt. 2:2)

For we have seen his star in its rising, and we have come *to worship* him [purpose].

μέλλει γὰρ Ἡρῴδης ζητεῖν τὸ παιδίον *τοῦ ἀπολέσαι* αὐτό. (Matt. 2:13)

For Herod is going to seek the child *in order to kill* him [purpose, with articular infinitive].

τότε διήνοιξεν αὐτῶν τὸν νοῦν *τοῦ συνιέναι* τὰς γραφάς. (Luke 24:45)

Then he opened their mind *so that they might understand* the Scriptures [result, though possibly purpose, with articular infinitive].

ὥστε *ἐξαπορηθῆναι* ἡμᾶς καὶ τοῦ ζῆν (2 Cor. 1:8)

So that we *despaired* even of living

> Result is indicated by the presence of the ὥστε before the infinitive ἐξαπορηθῆναι.

ἐνίκησεν ὁ λέων ὁ ἐκ τῆς φυλῆς Ἰούδα, ἡ ῥίζα Δαυίδ, ἀνοῖξαι τὸ βιβλίον καὶ τὰς ἑπτὰ σφραγῖδας αὐτοῦ. (Rev. 5:5)

The lion from the tribe of Judah, the root of David, has overcome *in order to/so as to open* the scroll and its seven seals.

> The infinitive filling the adverbial adjunct slot could express either the purpose or result of the process of overcoming.[17]

Articular Infinitive with a Preposition

A number of adverbial functions can be expressed with the infinitive following a preposition and an article: preposition + article + infinitive.[18] The articular infinitive functions as the object of the preposition (hence, its noun function), and the entire expression functions as an adverbial modifier to express a variety of adverbial notions dependent on the semantics of the preposition. The following chart summarizes the main constructions and their adverbial meanings.[19]

Prepositional construction	Meaning
μετὰ τό + infinitive: "after . . ." (subsequent) ἐν τῷ + infinitive: "when . . . ," "while . . ." (contemporary) πρὸ τοῦ (or πρίν [ἤ]) + infinitive: "before . . ." (antecedent)	Temporal
εἰς τό + infinitive: "in order that," "so that" πρὸς τό + infinitive: "in order that," "so that"	Purpose/result
διὰ τό + infinitive: "because"	Causal
ἐν τῷ + infinitive: "by"	Means

17. See Mathewson, *Revelation*, 73, for result but also other options.

18. Cf. von Siebenthal, *Ancient Greek Grammar*, 379–82.

19. This chart is a slight modification of Mathewson and Emig, *Intermediate Greek Grammar*, 198–99. Thanks are due to Elodie Emig for constructing this chart. Cf. also the chart in von Siebenthal, *Ancient Greek Grammar*, 380. Von Siebenthal (*Ancient Greek Grammar*, 380) notes that there is just one example each in the NT of the following prepositional constructions: ἀντί + genitive (James 4:15), showing substitution; διά + genitive (Heb. 2:15), functioning temporally; ἐκ + genitive (2 Cor. 8:11), functioning causally; ἕνεκεν + genitive (2 Cor. 7:12), expressing purpose; ἕως + genitive (Acts 8:40), functioning temporally.

Temporal

καὶ *ἐν τῷ σπείρειν αὐτὸν* ἃ μὲν ἔπεσεν παρὰ τὴν ὁδόν. (Matt. 13:4)

And *while/when* he *was sowing*, some fell along the way [contemporaneous].

Μετὰ δὲ *τὸ παραδοθῆναι τὸν* Ἰωάννην ἦλθεν ὁ Ἰησοῦς εἰς τὴν Γαλιλαίαν. (Mark 1:14)

And *after* John *was handed over*, Jesus came into Galilee [subsequent].

λέγει πρὸς αὐτὸν ὁ βασιλικός· κύριε, κατάβηθι *πρὶν ἀποθανεῖν τὸ παιδίον μου.* (John 4:49)

And the royal official said to him, "Lord, go down *before* my child *dies*" [antecedent].

δόξασόν με . . . τῇ δόξῃ ᾗ εἶχον *πρὸ τοῦ τὸν κόσμον εἶναι* παρὰ σοί. (John 17:5)

Glorify me . . . with the glory I had with you *before* the world *was* [antecedent].

In the above examples, the infinitive itself does not express temporal relationships. Rather, the preposition as a temporal deictic indicator establishes the temporal frame of reference.

Purpose/Result

ὁ βλέπων γυναῖκα *πρὸς τὸ ἐπιθυμῆσαι αὐτὴν* ἤδη ἐμοίχευσεν αὐτὴν ἐν τῇ καρδίᾳ αὐτοῦ. (Matt. 5:28)

The one who looks at a woman *in order to lust / so that he lusts* after her has already committed adultery with her in his heart.

> It is difficult to determine whether the act of looking is with the intention of getting a woman to lust, or whether looking at her in a certain way brings about the result of his lusting.

Μὴ οὖν βασιλευέτω ἡ ἁμαρτία ἐν τῷ θνητῷ ὑμῶν σώματι *εἰς τὸ ὑπακούειν* ταῖς ἐπιθυμίαις αὐτοῦ. (Rom. 6:12)

Therefore, sin should not reign in your mortal body *in order to obey* its desires.

Causal

ἔστιν δίκαιον ἐμοὶ τοῦτο φρονεῖν ὑπὲρ πάντων ὑμῶν διὰ τὸ ἔχειν με ἐν τῇ καρδίᾳ ὑμᾶς. (Phil. 1:7)

It is right for me to think this in behalf of all of you, *because* I *have* you in (my) heart.

> The causal construction functions as an adverbial adjunct modifying ἔστιν. For the translation adopted here, see the excursus, "The 'Subject' of the Infinitive," above. Notice also the infinitive φρονεῖν, which functions as the subject of ἔστιν.

οὐκ ἔχετε διὰ τὸ μὴ *αἰτεῖσθαι* ὑμᾶς. (James 4:2)

You do not have *because* you *do* not *ask.*

> The accusative pronoun ὑμᾶς functions as the subject of the negated infinitive.

Means

ἐν τῷ γὰρ ὑποτάξαι [αὐτῷ] τὰ πάντα οὐδὲν ἀφῆκεν αὐτῷ ἀνυπότακτον. (Heb. 2:8)

For *by subjecting* all things he left nothing not subjected to himself.

> The infinitive phrase ἐν τῷ γὰρ ὑποτάξαι fills the adverbial modifier slot, modifying the main verb ἀφῆκεν and indicating the means by which nothing was left subject.

Predicate Slot

Though not common in the New Testament, in some cases the infinitive can function as a finite verb and fill the syntactic slot of the predicate in a clause. In Porter's words, "An infinitive may be used in a predicate structure, serving the function of a finite verb such as an imperative (commanding use)."[20] Unlike the finite verb form that usually fills the syntactic slot of predicate, the infinitive does not contribute the features of mood, person, and number but merely states the verbal idea without presupposing its reality.

χαίρειν μετὰ χαιρόντων, κλαίειν μετὰ κλαιόντων. (Rom. 12:15)
Rejoice with those rejoicing, *weep* with those weeping.

> The two infinitives in the context follow imperatives in verse 14, and here the infinitives function as commands, filling the slot of an imperative in a main clause. While this could be understood as an infinitive modifying an elided finite verb form, it is preferable to analyze it as an infinitive filling the syntactical space of a finite verb, in this case functioning in a commanding sense.

ταῖς δώδεκα φυλαῖς ταῖς ἐν τῇ διασπορᾷ χαίρειν. (James 1:1)
To the twelve tribes in the dispersion, *greetings*.

> Porter notes that this is "a standard word of greeting used in the Hellenistic epistolary papyri discovered in Egypt."[21] The infinitive simply expresses the verbal idea and fills the slot of a main verb expressing a greeting. It could be a stereotyped expression.

Conclusion

The Greek infinitive exhibits a variety of functions, given its semantics of not presupposing the reality of the action in the verbal process but merely stating the verbal idea. In comparison to the mood forms of finite verbs, and in comparison to the participle, the infinitive is backgrounded in relationship to other verbal forms, since it makes no assertion or projection about reality, nor presupposes it like the participle, but only states the verbal idea. Furthermore, the infinitive is predominantly used in embedded constructions and

20. Porter, *Idioms*, 201.
21. Porter, *Idioms*, 202.

as a modifier or an adverbial adjunct, suggesting its secondary nature. In Romans 12:14–15 (see above) there is a contrast between
the directives to bless those who persecute rather than cursing them
(εὐλογεῖτε, μὴ καταρᾶσθε) in the imperative moods, and the commanding use of the infinitives (χαίρειν, κλαίειν), which does not presuppose the reality of the verbal processes but merely states the verbal
idea. Overall, the infinitive contributes to the interpersonal function
of the discourse.

Participles

The participle in its different functions is ubiquitous in the Greek of
the New Testament. As noted above, the Greek participle is often
defined as a verbal adjective, exhibiting features of both a verb and
an adjective. As a verb the participle grammaticalizes aspect, voice,
and number, but it is not limited by person. It occurs with the aorist, present, perfect (stative), and future forms, though the use of
the participle with the future was in decline by the time the New
Testament was being written. It also occurs with all three voice forms
(active, middle, passive). The participle can take adverbial modifiers
and can function as an adverbial modifier itself. As an adjective, the
participle takes case, gender, and number, which it gets from some
element in the larger context, and it can function in similar ways to
an adjective form. In certain syntactical environments, the participle
can take modifiers that a noun would take. More specifically, the
semantic contribution of the participle is presupposing the factual
status or reality of the action of the verb (Porter labels this +factive
presupposition).[22] That is, in differentiation from the infinitive, the
participle is used by an author to presuppose the reality of the state
of affairs indicated by the verb, whereas the infinitive makes no such
presupposition and merely states the verbal idea.

This brief introduction helps to explain the variety of usages of
the participle and the different syntactical environments in which it
appears in the Greek New Testament. Therefore, the participle can
at times fill the syntactical slot of a *noun* (substantive), such as the

22. Porter, *Verbal Aspect*, 391.

subject or direct object of a verb in a clause, or it can fill the syntactical slot of a *finite verb*. A very common usage of the participle is its function as a *modifier*. It can serve to modify a noun element in a text or a verbal element while functioning as an adverbial adjunct. Therefore, it is important to differentiate the *form* of the participle from the variety of *functions* it can fulfill. Most grammars analyze the participle according to its twofold adjectival and adverbial features, often with the independent use of the participle (functioning as a finite verb) receiving separate treatment.[23] Within these broad categories various subfunctions of the participle are discussed (e.g., under independent usage: as a finite verb, genitive absolute, periphrastic construction). The following classification is based on the two major syntactical functions of the participle either as a *modifier* of a noun (adjectival) or a verb (adverbial) or as an *independent element* such as a finite verb (including so-called genitive absolutes and periphrastic constructions) or a substantive. These various functions of the participle can be accounted for by the semantic feature of presupposing the reality or factual status of the state of affairs communicated by the participle form.

Another important factor in determining the grammatical function of the participle is the presence or absence of the article. The presence of an article (articular) indicates an adjectival function of a participle, either as a substantive (independent) or adjective modifier. However, both of these functions of the participle could still lack an article (anarthrous), though this is not as common, the determining factor being whether the participle occurs in the syntactical slot of a substantive or adjective modifier. The verbal functions of the participle, either as an adverbial modifier or as an independent verb form, will always lack the article (anarthrous) and will usually be in the nominative case form. However, the reverse is not necessarily true. While the presence of an article marks its adjectival function and is normal, the lack of an article does not guarantee its adverbial function, since anarthrous participles can still fulfill the syntactic roles of substantives (e.g., subject, object) or adjective modifiers, though this

---

23. Wallace, *Greek Grammar*, 617–53; Young, *Intermediate New Testament Greek*, 147–62; Black, *Still Greek to Me*, 122–24; Köstenberger, Merkle, and Plummer, *Going Deeper with New Testament Greek*, 324–44.

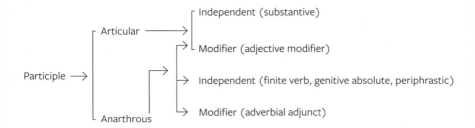

Figure 6.2

is less common.[24] Figure 6.2 above displays the four major participle functions discussed here and their relationship to the presence or absence of the article.

The Participle as Modifier

A very common function of the participle is its use as a modifying element, either modifying a substantive (adjectival) or a verb (adverbial adjunct). That is, the participle can fill the syntactic slot often occupied by other forms, such as adjectives or adverbs. The choice of the participle over these latter two forms allows the author to also communicate the verbal semantic features of aspect and voice.

Adjective Modifier (Attributive)

With or without an article, the participle can function as an adjective modifier and modify another substantive in a clause. This usage is common in the New Testament.

καὶ ὁ πατήρ σου ὁ βλέπων ἐν τῷ κρυφαίῳ ἀποδώσει σοι. (Matt. 6:18)
And your Father *who sees* in secret will reward you.

Οἱ μὲν οὖν διασπαρέντες ἀπὸ τῆς θλίψεως *τῆς γενομένης* ἐπὶ Στεφάνῳ (Acts 11:19)

24. "However, though the presence of the article guarantees that a participle is adjectival, the absence of the article does not guarantee that it is adverbial" (Mathewson and Emig, *Intermediate Greek Grammar*, 206).

Therefore, those who were scattered from the persecution *that happened* over Stephen

ἵνα μὴ λυπῆσθε καθὼς καὶ οἱ λοιποὶ *οἱ μὴ ἔχοντες* ἐλπίδα (1 Thess. 4:13)

In order that you might not grieve just as also the rest *who do not have* hope

Εὐλογητὸς ὁ θεὸς καὶ πατὴρ τοῦ κυρίου ἡμῶν Ἰησοῦ Χριστοῦ *ὁ κατὰ τὸ πολὺ αὐτοῦ ἔλεος ἀναγεννήσας* ἡμᾶς εἰς ἐλπίδα *ζῶσαν*. (1 Pet. 1:3)

Blessed is the God and Father of our Lord Jesus Christ, *who has given* us *new birth* according to his great mercy into a *living* hope.

> The first modifying participle is articular (ὁ... ἀναγεννήσας), whereas the second one is anarthrous (ζῶσαν).

καὶ οἱ λοιποὶ ἀπεκτάνθησαν ἐν τῇ ῥομφαίᾳ... *τῇ ἐξελθούσῃ ἐκ τοῦ στόματος αὐτοῦ.* (Rev. 19:21)

And the rest were killed by the sword, ... *which comes out of his mouth.*

Adverbial Adjunct

In an anarthrous construction, the participle can function as an adverbial adjunct, modifying another verb form in a clause (the so-called adverbial participle, or circumstantial participle). This use of the participle will be in the nominative case, since it is not only related to the verb but receives its case (also gender and number) from the stated or implied grammatical subject of the main verb it modifies. A common way of treating participles functioning in an adverbial manner is to provide a list of proposed adverbial functions of the participle with accompanying labels.[25]

---

25. This way of analyzing adverbial participles was standard fare in most older grammars as well. Cf. Dana and Mantey, *Manual Grammar*, 226–29; Blass and Debrunner, *Greek Grammar*, §418; Turner, *Syntax*, 3:153–58.

Porter notes that the "verb-modifying participle enters into a number of syntactical relations which have semantic consequences."[26] He lists the following possible relationships: concessive, causal, conditional, instrumental (manner or means), purpose (final), or result.[27] However, Porter recognizes that (1) these relationships can only be *inferred* from the context; and (2) "in some instances it may simply be better not to specify the relation between the participle and the other elements of the construction, since the context does not give specific indicators."[28] In his intermediate-level grammar, Black lists the following adverbial functions of the participle: temporal, causal, attendant circumstances, telic, conditional, concessive, instrumental.[29] Young lists the following ten functions: time, manner, means, reason, grounds, condition, concession, purpose, result, attendant circumstances.[30] In his extensive treatment of participles, Wallace's list deviates little from other standard lists in terms of functions and the labels assigned to them. He suggests the following "eight kinds of adverbial" functions: temporal, manner, means, cause, condition, concession, purpose (telic), result.[31] More recently, Köstenberger, Merkle, and Plummer provide a similar list of adverbial participle functions: temporal, means, manner, cause, condition, concession, purpose, result.[32] The more linguistically oriented grammar by von Siebenthal discerns the following six "adverbial nuances": temporal, manner, causal, concessive, conditional, purpose.[33] Yet he insists that such judgments are only inferable from context and thus that these judgments are somewhat flexible and that the native speaker was probably not aware of such distinctions.

While the employment of such stock labels and ostensible functions is commonplace in Greek grammars for interpreting participles that function as adverbial adjuncts, when we pay closer attention

26. Porter, *Idioms*, 190.
27. Porter, *Idioms*, 191–93.
28. Porter, *Idioms*, 191.
29. Black, *Still Greek to Me*, 122–23.
30. Young, *Intermediate New Testament Greek*, 153–59.
31. Wallace, *Greek Grammar*, 623–40.
32. Köstenberger, Merkle, and Plummer, *Going Deeper with New Testament Greek*, 327–35.
33. Von Siebenthal, *Ancient Greek Grammar*, 391–99.

to the nuances that derive from broader contextual relations, the following criticisms can be made of this approach. First, as some of the above grammars recognize, these functional labels do not belong to the semantics of the participle, nor are they different types of participles, but rather they can only be *inferred* from the context, if at all. Thus, Wallace incorrectly labels these as "eight kinds of adverbial participles."[34] Second, this raises the further issue of how we understand context, the relationship between the participle and its context, and the basis on which we make such inferences. For example, in his discussion of the adverbial participle in Ephesians 5:19–21, Wallace ultimately points to broader Pauline theology as to why some labels don't fit, and why *result* is the best option.[35] The only grammatical clue he can point to is the fact that the participles follow the main verb they modify, though this is not unique to a participle of result. Thus, one's theological perspective can influence or even determine which descriptive label is chosen. But as Porter recognizes, the context of the participle often does not give specific indicators, making the use of such labels problematic. As a verbal form that communicates the author's desire to presuppose the reality of the action, these further nuances are not grammaticalized by the participle, so it is incorrect to attribute them to the semantics of the participle and see these as different "kinds of participles." These meanings are present only in the broader context, if at all, and often the context is ambiguous regarding these semantic notions, so that it is usually better not to indicate one of these relationships apart from compelling evidence.

Third, the participle is indeterminate for these meanings and is not marked for such semantic nuances as time, manner, cause, condition, concession, and so on. Further, if the author wanted to communicate such features, he or she had clearer means of doing so, especially clauses introduced by conjunctives: for example, ὅτι (cause), ἵνα/ὅπως (purpose), ὥστε (result), ὅτε/ὅταν (temporal), εἰ/ἐάν (conditional), and ὡς/καθώς/ὥσπερ (manner), among others. The participle

34. Wallace, *Greek Grammar*, 639.
35. Wallace, *Greek Grammar*, 639. Wallace says there are other factors that support this view, but he does not mention what they are or provide discussion of them.

itself does not communicate such nuances. As Porter suggests, often the context is ambiguous so that it is better not to specify these meanings.[36] Additionally, McKay says, "Indeed the use of a participle produces an ambiguity which the writer no doubt saw as preferable to selection of one of the different clause types which might have been appropriate to the context."[37] Therefore, Mathewson and Emig conclude that "a participle seems to be the ideal construction to use when the author does not want to commit to any specific adverbial meaning (cause, manner, condition, etc.)."[38]

How, then, should adverbial participles be analyzed?[39] A more important observation is the structural position of the participle in relation to the main verb and the temporal and logical information they convey. A key factor in analyzing participles is their position in relationship to the nuclear verb that they modify, whether they *precede* or *follow* the modified verb.[40] When an adverbial participle precedes the main verb, it tends to refer to action prior to the main verb temporally and logically.[41] When the participle follows the main verb, it tends to indicate contemporaneous or subsequent action to that of the main verb.[42] This pattern appears to hold in a large number of examples in the New Testament. At the end of the day, each context should be carefully analyzed to establish the temporal frame of reference of adverbial participles.[43] A further corollary of this temporal ordering is the logical notion entailed by the structural relation of the participle to the main verb. When the adverbial participle precedes the main verb, it indicates secondary, background, or

36. Porter, *Idioms*, 191.

37. McKay, *New Syntax*, 61.

38. Mathewson and Emig, *Intermediate Greek Grammar*, 211.

39. The following section is heavily dependent upon Mathewson and Emig, *Intermediate Greek Grammar*, 211–16.

40. This is in contrast to approaches that rely on the aspect of the participle, whether aorist or present, to determine logical and temporal relationships.

41. Porter, *Verbal Aspect*, 381: "When the Participle is placed before the main verb, there is a tendency for the action depicted to be antecedent." Cf. Porter, *Idioms*, 188; Mathewson and Emig, *Intermediate Greek Grammar*, 217.

42. Porter, *Verbal Aspect*, 381: "When the Participle is placed after the main verb, there is a tendency for the action to be seen as concurrent or subsequent." Cf. Porter, *Idioms*, 188.

43. Mathewson and Emig, *Intermediate Greek Grammar*, 219.

prerequisite action to that of the modified verb.[44] "This means that the information they [adverbial participles] convey is of secondary importance vis-à-vis that of the nuclear clause."[45] Conversely, when the participle follows the main verb, the participle as an adverbial adjunct tends to further define or explain the action of the main verb or indicate what the action of the verb entails. In other words, it can elaborate on the action of the main verb, explaining what it means.[46] Therefore, adverbial participles either provide secondary information or they further explain and elaborate on the action of the primary verbs in a clause. Any further information, such as cause, manner, time, concession, and so on, depends on other contextual indicators and is not the most important feature of the participle; it should probably be given less attention in exegesis.

καὶ *ἀνοίξαντες* τοὺς θησαυροὺς αὐτῶν προσήνεγκαν αὐτῷ δῶρα, χρυσὸν καὶ λίβανον καὶ σμύρναν. (Matt. 2:11)

And *opening* their treasures they offered him gifts, gold and incense and myrrh.

> The adverbial participle precedes the main verb and indicates action that is temporally prior to the main verb of "offered," and logically it indicates a prerequisite step to the action of the main verb. The participle indicates background and secondary information (irrespective of how we translate it).

πορευθέντες οὖν μαθητεύσατε πάντα τὰ ἔθνη, βαπτίζοντες αὐτοὺς εἰς τὸ ὄνομα τοῦ πατρὸς καὶ τοῦ υἱοῦ καὶ τοῦ ἁγίου πνεύματος, διδάσκοντες αὐτοὺς τηρεῖν πάντα ὅσα ἐνετειλάμην ὑμῖν. (Matt. 28:19–20)

44. According to Young, the participle can enter into a step-GOAL relationship with the verb in the main clause (*Intermediate New Testament Greek*, 158). That is, the action in the participle provides a necessary step to achieving the main goal, which is the action of the main verb.
45. Levinsohn, *Discourse Features of New Testament Greek*, 183.
46. Runge, *Discourse Grammar of the Greek New Testament*, 262.

Therefore, *having gone*, make disciples of all nations, *baptizing* them in the name of the Father and the Son and the Holy Spirit, and *teaching* them to keep all that I have commanded you.

> The main verb, an imperative μαθητεύσατε, is both preceded and followed by participles functioning as adverbial adjuncts. The participle that precedes, πορευθέντες, gives temporally prior information but also secondary, background information to the main verb. The two participles following the main verb, βαπτίζοντες and διδάσκοντες, indicate temporally contemporaneous action and provide further explanation of what the action of making disciples entails.[47]

ἐν αὐτῷ περιπατεῖτε, *ἐρριζωμένοι* καὶ *ἐποικοδομούμενοι* ἐν αὐτῷ καὶ *βεβαιούμενοι* τῇ πίστει καθὼς ἐδιδάχθητε, *περισσεύοντες* ἐν εὐχαριστίᾳ. (Col. 2:6–7)

Walk in him, *being rooted* and *being built up* in him, *being strengthened* in the faith just as you were taught, *abounding* in thanksgiving.

> The four adverbial participles follow the main verb περιπατεῖτε and so provide contemporaneous action to the main verb and elaborate on it, providing further explanation of what the imperative "walk" entails.

οὐδεὶς *στρατευόμενος* ἐμπλέκεται ταῖς τοῦ βίου πραγματείαις. (2 Tim. 2:4)

No one *serving as a soldier* gets involved in the matters of life.

> The adverbial participle precedes the main verb and so provides secondary, prerequisite information to the main verb. This may be an example of where the participle preceding the main verb refers to concurrent action with that of the verb it modifies.

47. Cf. for further details, Mathewson and Emig, *Intermediate Greek Grammar*, 212, 214; Porter, *Linguistic Analysis of the Greek New Testament*, 245.

καθαρισμὸν τῶν ἁμαρτιῶν *ποιησάμενος* ἐκάθισεν ἐν δεξιᾷ τῆς μεγαλωσύνης ἐν ὑψηλοῖς. (Heb. 1:3)

Having made purification for sins, he sat down at the right hand of the majesty on high.

> The act of making purification is temporally prior to the main verb ἐκάθισεν and gives secondary, background information.

Καὶ ἀπεκρίθη εἷς ἐκ τῶν πρεσβυτέρων *λέγων* μοι (Rev. 7:13)

And one of the elders answered, *saying* to me

> Though sometimes labeled a "redundant" or "pleonastic" participle construction, it is better to see the adverbial adjunct λέγων following the main verb as temporally contemporaneous and further specifying what is entailed in the main verb ἀπεκρίθη, introducing the content of the elder's answer.

The Independent Participle

Verbal

The participle may occur in a variety of contexts where it functions as an independent verb form. The following examples amply illustrate this function.

Predicate

Though not common, in this usage the participle fills the syntactic slot of a main, finite verb, usually functioning as a command. Though this is often attributed to the presence of an elided verb that the participle presumably modifies, it is better to understand the following examples as independent uses of the participle functioning as main verbs in the clause.[48] Often the participle functions in an imperatival sense, but there are also examples of the participle functioning like an indicative verb.

48. Porter, *Idioms*, 185–86.

ἀλλὰ καὶ *καυχώμενοι* ἐν τῷ θεῷ διὰ τοῦ κυρίου ἡμῶν Ἰησοῦ Χριστοῦ.
(Rom. 5:11)
But also (we) *boast* in God through our Lord Jesus Christ.

Ἡ ἀγάπη ἀνυπόκριτος. *ἀποστυγοῦντες* τὸ πονηρόν, *κολλώμενοι* τῷ
ἀγαθῷ. (Rom. 12:9; cf. vv. 10–19)
Love (must be) without hypocrisy. *Hate* what is evil; *cling to* what
is good.

Οἱ οἰκέται *ὑποτασσόμενοι* ἐν παντὶ φόβῳ τοῖς δεσπόταις. (1 Pet. 2:18;
cf. 1:14)[49]
Servants, *submit* in all fear to your masters.

καὶ τὸ τεῖχος τῆς πόλεως *ἔχων* θεμελίους δώδεκα. (Rev. 21:14)[50]
And the wall of the city *had* twelve foundations.

Genitive Absolute

As the designation for this participle usage implies, the participle
functions as an independent element in an absolute construction. "An
absolute construction means that the participle is not formally dependent upon any other sentence or sentence element."[51] Therefore, Young
is not entirely correct in analyzing the genitive absolute construction
as a subordinate adverbial clause that modifies the verb of a main
clause.[52] However, though grammatically independent, the genitive
absolute construction is *conceptually* related to the main clause, and
the subject of the absolute construction is sometimes picked up with
a noun in another case in the main clause (cf. Matt. 8:1: Καταβάντος
δὲ <u>αὐτοῦ</u> ἀπὸ τοῦ ὄρους ἠκολούθησαν <u>αὐτῷ</u> ὄχλοι πολλοί [But *when*
<u>he</u> *came down* from the mountain, great crowds followed <u>him</u>]). In
the genitive absolute construction, the participle and its subject (if

---

49. See Dubis, *1 Peter*, 71.
50. Mathewson, *Revelation*, 292. Revelation may have a number of other examples
of the participle functioning as a finite verb.
51. Porter, *Idioms*, 183.
52. Young, *Intermediate New Testament Greek*, 159. The independent function of
the genitive absolute is irrespective of how we translate it. Often it will be translated
as a dependent participle functioning as an adverbial adjunct (see above). However, it
still functions as an independent verb, even if conceptually related to the main clause.

present) occur in the genitive case, marking the fact that the subject of the genitive participle is different from the subject of the verb in the main clause. In the example from Matthew 8:1 above, the subject of the participle in the genitive absolute construction (αὐτοῦ) is different from the subject of the main verb ἠκολούθησαν, the crowds (ὄχλοι πολλοί). The genitive absolute normally occurs at the beginning of a clausal unit. Genitive absolute constructions serve to indicate a transition of some kind into a new topic or scene or into the introduction of a new participant. This device is often known as a "switch reference."[53]

Ἀναχωρησάντων δὲ αὐτῶν ἰδοὺ ἄγγελος κυρίου φαίνεται κατ᾽ ὄναρ τῷ Ἰωσήφ. (Matt. 2:13)
And *when they had departed*, behold an angel of the Lord appeared in a dream to Joseph.

> The genitive absolute functions to provide a transition from the departing of the magi to a new scene where an angel appears to Joseph.

Τῶν δὲ ὄχλων ἐπαθροιζομένων ἤρξατο λέγειν. (Luke 11:29)
And the *crowds increasing*, he [Jesus] began to speak.

Ἔτι λαλοῦντος τοῦ Πέτρου τὰ ῥήματα ταῦτα ἐπέπεσεν τὸ πνεῦμα τὸ ἅγιον ἐπὶ πάντας τοὺς ἀκούοντας τὸν λόγον. (Acts 10:44)
While *Peter was still speaking* these words, the Holy Spirit fell upon all who heard the message.

ἐποικοδομηθέντες ἐπὶ τῷ θεμελίῳ τῶν ἀποστόλων καὶ προφητῶν, ὄντος ἀκρογωνιαίου αὐτοῦ Χριστοῦ Ἰησοῦ (Eph. 2:20)
Being built upon the foundation of the apostles and prophets, *Jesus Christ* himself *being* the chief cornerstone

> The genitive absolute here occurs *after* the main clause, probably for emphasis.

53. Levinsohn, *Discourse Features of New Testament Greek*, 182; cf. Mathewson and Emig, *Intermediate Greek Grammar*, 221; Young, *Intermediate New Testament Greek*, 159.

Χριστοῦ οὖν παθόντος σαρκὶ καὶ ὑμεῖς τὴν αὐτὴν ἔννοιαν ὁπλίσασθε.
(1 Pet. 4:1)

Therefore, *Christ having suffered* in the flesh, you also arm your-selves with the same insight.

> The genitive absolute provides a switch to a new subject (ὑμεῖς) where the implications of Christ's suffering are now drawn out for the readers.

Periphrastic

Two further participle constructions can be considered here as functioning in a predicate capacity (similar to a main verb), though they could also be treated under other functions of the participle. They are not so much independent uses, but together with another verb create a complex that functions as a verbal unit.

The first of these two constructions is the periphrastic construction. A periphrastic construction consists of two elements: (1) an auxiliary verb, usually εἰμί or sometimes γίνομαι, and (2) a participle that immediately precedes or follows the auxiliary verb, with only modifiers and adjuncts coming in between the two elements.[54] Together these two elements constitute the periphrastic construction, which communicates the verbal process in a clause. Von Siebenthal treats periphrastic constructions under the heading of predicative participle and describes it as a "multi-part predicator."[55] This use of the participle could be seen as an adjectival usage, though it still contributes the verbal notions of aspect and voice to the construction. The auxiliary verb communicates the features of person and attitude (mood), while the participle communicates the semantic features of aspect and voice. In periphrastic constructions the participle occurs only in the present (imperfective) and perfect (stative) aspects. For most finite verb forms a periphrastic construction can be substituted (see below). The periphrastic construction, in relation to a finite verb, probably functions to draw attention to the participle and its modifiers; it is a more semantically significant construction.[56] At times a

---

54. Porter, *Verbal Aspect*, 453.
55. Von Siebenthal, *Ancient Greek Grammar*, 404.
56. Porter, *Idioms*, 46.

periphrastic construction may serve to substitute for a simple verb form that is dying out (e.g., the imperfect of εἰμί + a perfect participle for the pluperfect form). The following constructions can be found in the New Testament.

Present periphrastic (for present tense form): present tense εἰμί + present participle

καὶ ἐγενόμην νεκρὸς καὶ ἰδοὺ ζῶν *εἰμι* εἰς τοὺς αἰῶνας τῶν αἰώνων. (Rev. 1:18)

And I was dead, and behold I *am living* forever and ever.

> In this text the participle precedes the auxiliary verb εἰμί.

Imperfect periphrastic (for imperfect tense form): imperfect tense εἰμί + present participle

ἤμην δὲ *ἀγνοούμενος* τῷ προσώπῳ ταῖς ἐκκλησίαις τῆς Ἰουδαίας. (Gal. 1:22)

But I *was unknown* by face to the churches of Judea.

Future periphrastic (for future tense form): future tense εἰμί + present participle

καὶ *ἔσεσθε μισούμενοι* ὑπὸ πάντων τῶν ἐθνῶν διὰ τὸ ὄνομά μου. (Matt. 24:9)

And you *will be hated* by all the nations on account of my name.

Perfect periphrastic (for perfect tense form): present tense εἰμί + perfect participle

χάριτί *ἐστε σεσῳσμένοι* . . . Τῇ γὰρ χάριτί *ἐστε σεσῳσμένοι* διὰ πίστεως. (Eph. 2:5, 8)

By grace you *are saved.* . . . For by grace you *are saved* through faith.

Pluperfect periphrastic (for pluperfect tense form): imperfect tense εἰμί + perfect participle

καὶ ἡ γυνὴ *ἦν περιβεβλημένη* πορφυροῦν καὶ κόκκινον. (Rev. 17:4)

And the woman *was clothed* in purple and scarlet.

> As already noted, the pluperfect periphrastic construction
> is substituting for the simple pluperfect form in the New
> Testament, with the latter form dying out.

Future perfect periphrastic (no corresponding simple form): future
tense εἰμί + perfect participle

καὶ ὃ ἐὰν δήσῃς ἐπὶ τῆς γῆς ἔσται δεδεμένον ἐν τοῖς οὐρανοῖς, καὶ ὃ
ἐὰν λύσῃς ἐπὶ τῆς γῆς ἔσται λελυμένον ἐν τοῖς οὐρανοῖς. (Matt.
16:19; cf. 18:18)

And whatever you bind upon the earth *will be bound* in heaven,
and whatever you loose upon the earth *will be loosed* in heaven.

> This is one of the best-known occurrences of this con-
> struction in the New Testament, and one with potential
> important theological ramifications.[57] The interpretive
> question concerns whether the earthly binding and loosing
> is determinative for the heavenly counterparts, or whether
> the earthly binding and loosing merely ratifies what has
> already taken place in heaven. The future perfect peri-
> phrastic construction only expects a future state of affairs,
> which does not necessarily entail that the heavenly binding
> and loosing is completely contingent on the corresponding
> earthly acts.[58]

The following two examples demonstrate how the auxiliary verb
indicates mood in the periphrastic construction.

Subjunctive: subjunctive of εἰμί + perfect participle

ἵνα μὴ πεποιθότες ὦμεν ἐφ᾽ ἑαυτοῖς ἀλλ᾽ ἐπὶ τῷ θεῷ (2 Cor. 1:9)

In order that we *might rely* not upon ourselves but upon God [with
the auxiliary verb following the participle][59]

57. Porter, "Vague Verbs."
58. See Mathewson and Emig, *Intermediate Greek Grammar*, 224–25.
59. The only example of a possible periphrastic construction with a present participle is James 1:4: ἵνα ἦτε τέλειοι καὶ ὁλόκληροι ἐν μηδενὶ λειπόμενοι (in order that you
might be perfect and *complete, lacking* in nothing).

Imperative: imperative of εἰμί + present participle

Ἴσθι εὐνοῶν τῷ ἀντιδίκῳ σου ταχύ, ἕως ὅτου εἶ μετ' αὐτοῦ ἐν τῇ ὁδῷ. (Matt. 5:25)

Be friends with your adversary quickly while you are with them on the way.

Supplementary (Complementary)

"The complementary or supplementary use of the participle occurs when the idea of the finite verb is completed by the participle."[60] That is, the participle "completes the meaning and syntactical structure of the predicate."[61] Both elements (predicate and participle) constitute a single syntactical unit. By completing the idea of a finite verb, the participle can be seen along with the finite verb as functioning to convey the verbal notion in a clause. It would also be possible to see the participle as functioning substantivally as the complement or object of the verb (see below).[62] The complementary participle usually occurs with a verb of ceasing (παύω) or completing (τελέω).[63]

Καὶ ἐγένετο ὅτε ἐτέλεσεν ὁ Ἰησοῦς διατάσσων τοῖς δώδεκα μαθηταῖς αὐτοῦ (Matt. 11:1)

And it came about when Jesus finished *instructing* his twelve disciples

οὐκ ἐπαύοντο διδάσκοντες καὶ εὐαγγελιζόμενοι τὸν χριστὸν Ἰησοῦν. (Acts 5:42)

And they did not cease *teaching* and *preaching* Christ Jesus.

οὐ παυόμεθα ὑπὲρ ὑμῶν προσευχόμενοι καὶ αἰτούμενοι. (Col. 1:9)

We do not cease *praying* on your behalf and *asking*.

Substantival

Grammaticalizing the feature of presupposing the factual status of the process, the participle can function to fill the slot of a noun or

60. Porter, *Idioms*, 192.
61. Young, *Intermediate New Testament Greek*, 149.
62. Young, *Intermediate New Testament Greek*, 149–50.
63. Wallace, *Greek Grammar*, 646; Young, *Intermediate New Testament Greek*, 149.

substantive in a clause, functioning syntactically in a variety of ways that a noun can. Its function determines its case, gender, and number. Unlike a noun form, the participle functioning in this manner also communicates the features of aspect and voice.

μὴ φοβηθῆτε ἀπὸ τῶν ἀποκτεινόντων τὸ σῶμα. (Luke 12:4)
Do not be afraid of *those who kill* the body.

> The participle in the genitive case functions as the object of the preposition ἀπό.

οἱ γὰρ κατὰ σάρκα ὄντες τὰ τῆς σαρκὸς φρονοῦσιν. (Rom. 8:5)
For *those who are* according to the flesh think the things belonging to the flesh [subject of the verb φρονοῦσιν].

ἡ γὰρ κρίσις ἀνέλεος τῷ μὴ ποιήσαντι ἔλεος. (James 2:13)
For judgment without mercy (will be) to anyone *who does* not *do* mercy [dative recipient of an assumed verb].

οὗτός ἐστιν ὁ ἀντίχριστος, ὁ ἀρνούμενος τὸν πατέρα καὶ τὸν υἱόν. (1 John 2:22)
This is the antichrist, *the one who denies* the Father and the Son.

> The nominative participle construction ὁ ἀρνούμενος stands in appositional relationship to the demonstrative pronoun οὗτος.

πᾶς ὁ ἀγαπῶν τὸν γεννήσαντα ἀγαπᾷ καὶ τὸν γεγεννημένον ἐξ αὐτοῦ. (1 John 5:1)
Everyone who loves *the one who gives birth* also loves *the one who is born* from him.

> Both participles in the accusative case fill the syntactic slot of direct object of the verbal processes (note that the first instance is a direct object of a participle itself [ὁ ἀγαπῶν]).

Καὶ ἤκουσα τὸν ἀριθμὸν *τῶν ἐσφραγισμένων*, ἑκατὸν τεσσεράκοντα τέσσαρες χιλιάδες. (Rev. 7:4)

And I heard the number *of those who were sealed*, one hundred
and forty-four thousand.

> The participle in the genitive fills the slot of a substantive
> and restricts the head term τὸν ἀριθμόν.

Conclusion

The participle, as a form that grammaticalizes the semantic feature
of presupposing the factive status of a verbal process, like the infinitive is a nonfinite verbal form and functions in a variety of syntactical
roles. These can be discussed under modifying (adjectival, adverbial
adjunct) and independent (verbal and substantival) roles. It is helpful
to see these as different syntactical spaces or slots in which the participle can be used (along with other forms, e.g., adjectives, adverbs,
substantives, finite verbs). The presence or absence of the article plays
an important role in determining the function of a participle. The
participle can contribute to the ideational function of language by
indicating the verbal processes that contribute to the textual repre-
sentation of reality. But perhaps more specifically they contribute to
the interpersonal metafunction of language in expressing the author's
role in relationship to the audience. Unlike the mood forms, which
express attitudinal features, such as assertion and nonassertion, the
participle does not make any assertion about reality but refers to factive presupposition in relationship to the verbal process. That is, the
biblical author further distances himself from assertions regarding
reality. The participle seems to indicate background information in
relationship to the indicative and nonindicative mood forms. It is primarily used in secondary and embedded clauses. At times participles
can be used to express some of the main speech functions (see chap.
5 above), such as command.

CONCLUSION

The preceding chapters have considered in some detail two important semantic features of the Greek verb in the New Testament: voice and mood. Like verbal aspect, the features of voice and mood are grammaticalized in the verb morphology (endings). Though verbal aspect is probably the most important feature communicated by the verb, voice and mood convey vital information related to the author's conception of the verbal processes in the text. Voice grammaticalizes the author's portrayal of the action in terms of the role of the grammatical subject as it relates to causality and agency. Mood indicates the author's conception of the verbal process as it relates to reality, indicating different attitudinal semantic features. Seen in this way, like verbal aspect both voice and mood are subjective, in that they indicate the author's perspective on the process in terms of causality and relation to reality. Furthermore, both are to be seen systemically as a network of choices available to the author as part of the larger language system, so that each feature in the voice or mood system is to be understood in relation to the others rather than in isolation. When the author is choosing how to portray a verbal process, the choice of both voice and mood is obligatory.

We have defined voice in the Greek of the New Testament as the author's conception of a verbal process in terms of the role of the grammatical subject as it relates to causality and agency. Thus, a description of the semantics of voice includes two related features: (1) the portrayal of causality and agency; (2) the role of the grammatical subject. Therefore, based on the feature of causality, three different voices can be distinguished: active, middle, and passive. Morphologically, while the imperfective and stative aspects reflect formal syncretization for the middle and passive, the aorist and future forms have separate endings that distinguish middle and passive voice. The -(θ)η- generally distinguishes the passive voice in the aorist and future, though there may be times where it extends to cover middle meanings. For the imperfective and stative aspects the middle and passive voices are contextually determined (e.g., the presence of a prepositional phrase).

The active voice in Greek encodes direct causality, and the subject is portrayed as the direct agent of the action in the verbal process. As the most commonly occurring voice in the Greek of the New Testament the active voice is the unmarked voice form, simply presenting the process from the standpoint of direct causality and the subject as the agent of the verbal process. By contrast, both the passive and middle voices present the grammatical subject as the medium, the entity affected by the verbal process (the direct object in an active-voice construction). What distinguishes the two is where causality lies in relationship to the verbal process. Reflecting linguistic studies on ergativity (e.g., SFL), the middle voice grammaticalizes internal causality. That is, the cause of the action arises from within, more specifically, from within the medium + verb complex. The middle voice, then, indicates ergativity. In contrast, the passive voice grammaticalizes indirect external causality, so that cause and agency occur outside the medium + subject complex, expressed by a prepositional phrase, if explicit. The middle and passive voices are less common in frequency than the active voice, and hence are more marked constructions, with the middle voice often offering the most significant choice. A group of verbs often (mis)labeled as "deponent verbs" (e.g., ἔρχομαι) does not offer a formal choice in the active voice. Rather than resorting to the label "deponent," we should see such verbs as true middles, grammaticalizing internal causality (some call these "middle-only" verbs). Voice contributes to the ideational metafunction of a text, indicating how the author conceives of the participants and their relationship to the verbal process and causality.

We defined mood (modality) in the Greek of the New Testament above as the author's conception of a process as it relates to reality.

The moods in Greek are not to be seen as indicating objective reality and factuality; rather, they indicate the author's subjective portrayal of the action's relation to reality (whether it reflects objective reality or not, though it can be used to do so in, e.g., narrative). The mood system in Greek can be broken down broadly into assertive (epistemic) and nonassertive (deontic) moods. The assertive mood corresponds to the indicative mood, while within the nonassertive mood further nuances can be distinguished. The nonassertive mood consists of three further moods that have in common the fact that they make no assertion about the action's relation to reality but rather indicate volition or deontic modality. The subjunctive mood grammaticalizes the semantic feature of projection or visualization, projecting a hypothetical reality for consideration. This feature accounts for its various functions and speech roles. Notions such as likelihood of fulfillment or levels of certainty are not part of the semantics of the subjunctive mood form. The optative mood grammaticalizes the semantic features of projection, or visualization, and contingency. That is, the action in the process is seen as contingent on other factors and is used for statements or questions that are more hesitant from the standpoint of the author. For various reasons, this form is restricted in usage in the Greek of the New Testament. Finally, the imperative mood grammaticalizes the semantic feature of direction; that is, the author directs the actions of the readers, so the imperative could be seen as the farthest removed from making assertions about reality (indicative). The most common function of the imperative form is in commands and prohibitions. The future tense form, while not technically a mood, could be seen in relation to the other moods as grammaticalizing the feature of expectation. Mood in Greek contributes to the interpersonal metafunction (the role of the author in relationship to the readers) of the text and also contributes to the performance of various speech roles (e.g., assertive statements, assertive questions, projective statements, projective contingent questions, etc.).

Two further forms and their functions have been considered along with the moods, though they do not technically grammaticalize attitudinal features as part of the mood system in Greek: infinitives and participles. Participles are seen to indicate the semantic feature of presupposing factual status of the process. This feature seems to account for its various functions in both dependent and independent constructions. By contrast, the infinitive does not presuppose the factual status of the process but only states the verbal ideal. Hence, it often conveys background information in relationship to the participle and the mood forms. This understanding of the infinitive best accounts for its variety of functions.

There is more work to be done on a number of issues relating to voice and mood, such as testing whether causality provides a unifying semantic description for the Greek voice forms, or further examining how mood relates to the various speech functions in Greek. However, this monograph has attempted to make suggestive observations on the semantics and function of the voices and moods as part of a system of semantic choices within the language system of Greek. Overall, a careful consideration of voice and mood in the Greek New Testament presents the interpreter with several important decisions in analyzing the verbal processes in any given text.

BIBLIOGRAPHY

Adam, A. K. M. *James: A Handbook on the Greek Text*. Waco: Baylor, 2013.

Aland, Barbara, Kurt Aland, Johannes Karavidopoulos, Carlo M. Martini, and Bruce M. Metzger, eds. *The Greek New Testament*. 5th rev. ed. Stuttgart: United Bible Societies, 2014.

Allan, Rutger J. *The Middle Voice in Ancient Greek: A Study in Polesemy*. Amsterdam Studies in Ancient Philology. Leiden: Brill, 2003.

Aubrey, Rachel. "Motivated Categories, Middle Voice, and Passive Morphology." In *The Greek Verb Revisited: A Fresh Approach for Biblical Exegesis*, edited by Steven E. Runge and Christopher J. Fresch, 563–625. Bellingham: Lexham Press, 2016.

Berry, Margaret. "The Clause: An Overview of the Lexicogrammar." In Thompson et al., *The Cambridge Handbook of Systemic Functional Linguistics*, 92–117.

Black, David Alan. *It's Still Greek to Me: An Easy-to-Understand Guide to Intermediate Greek*. Grand Rapids: Baker, 1998.

———. *Linguistics for Students of New Testament Greek*. 2nd ed. Grand Rapids: Baker, 1988.

Blass, Friedrich, and Albert Debrunner. *A Greek Grammar of the New Testament and Other Early Christian Literature*. Translated and edited by Robert A. Funk. Chicago: University of Chicago Press, 1961.

Boyer, James L. "The Classification of Imperatives: A Statistical Study." *Grace Theological Journal* 8 (1987): 35–54.

———. "The Classification of Optatives: A Statistical Study." *Grace Theological Journal* 9 (1988): 129–40.

———. "The Classification of Subjunctives: A Statistical Study." *Grace Theological Journal* 7 (1986): 3–19.

————. "First Class Conditions: What Do They Mean?" *Grace Theological Journal* 2, no. 1 (1981): 75–114.

Callow, Kathleen. "Patterns of Thematic Development in 1 Corinthians 5:1–13." In *Linguistics and New Testament Interpretation: Essays on Discourse Analysis*, edited by David Alan Black, 194–206. Nashville: Broadman, 1992.

Campbell, Constantine R. *Advances in the Study of Greek: New Insights for Reading the New Testament*. Grand Rapids: Zondervan, 2015.

————. *Verbal Aspect in Non-Indicative Verbs: Further Soundings in the Greek of the New Testament*. New York: Peter Lang, 2008.

Carson, D. A. *Exegetical Fallacies*. 2nd ed. Grand Rapids: Baker, 1996.

Clackson, James. *Indo-European Linguistics: An Introduction*. Cambridge Textbooks in Linguistics. Cambridge: Cambridge University Press, 2007.

Collins COBUILD English Grammar. London: Collins, 1990.

Culy, Martin M. "Double Accusative Case Constructions in Koine Greek." *Journal of Greco-Roman Christianity and Judaism* 6 (2009): 82–106.

Dana, H. E., and Julius Mantey. *A Manual Grammar of the Greek New Testament*. Toronto: MacMillan, 1955.

Decker, Rodney J. *Reading Koine Greek*. Grand Rapids: Baker Academic, 2014.

Dixon, R. M. W. "Ergativity." *Language* 55 (March 1979): 59–138.

Donovan, J. "Sonnenschein's Greek Grammar." *Classical Review* 9 (1895): 60–67.

Dubis, Mark. *1 Peter: A Handbook on the Greek Text*. Waco: Baylor, 2010.

Dvorak, James. "'Evidence That Commands a Verdict': Determining the Semantics of Imperatives in the New Testament." *Biblical and Ancient Greek Linguistics* 7 (2018): 201–23.

Evans, Vyvyan. *Cognitive Linguistics: A Complete Guide*. Edinburgh: Edinburgh University Press, 2019.

Fanning, Buist M. *Verbal Aspect in New Testament Greek*. Oxford: Clarendon, 1990.

Fantin, Joseph D. *The Greek Imperative Mood in the New Testament: A Cognitive and Communicative Approach*. Studies in Biblical Greek 12. New York: Peter Lang, 2010.

————. "May the *Force* Be with You: Volition, Direction, and Force; A Communicative Approach to the Imperative Mood." *Biblical and Ancient Greek Linguistics* 7 (2018): 173–99.

Fletcher, Bryan W. Y. "Voice in the Greek of the New Testament." PhD diss., McMaster Divinity College, 2020.

Friberg, Barbara, and Timothy Friberg, eds. *Analytical Greek New Testament*. Grand Rapids: Baker, 1981.

Gonda, J. *The Character of the Indo-European Moods*. Wiesbaden: Otto Harrassowitz, 1956.

Halliday, M. A. K. *Explorations in the Functions of Language*. London: Edward Arnold, 1973.

———. *An Introduction to Functional Grammar*. London: Edward Arnold, 1985.

———. *Language as Social Semiotic: The Social Interpretation of Language and Meaning*. London: Edward Arnold, 1978.

Halliday, M. A. K., and Christian M. I. M. Matthiessen. *An Introduction to Functional Grammar*. 3rd ed. London: Edward Arnold, 2004.

Harris, Dana M. "The Study of the Greek Language." In *The State of New Testament Studies: A Survey of Recent Research*, edited by Scot McKnight and Nijay K. Gupta, 132–36. Grand Rapids: Baker Academic, 2019.

Hopper, Paul J., and Sandra A. Thompson. "Transitivity in Grammar and Discourse." *Language* 56, no. 2 (1980): 251–99.

Huffman, Douglas S. *Verbal Aspect Theory and the Prohibitions in the Greek New Testament*. Studies in Biblical Greek 16. New York: Peter Lang, 2014.

Jongkind, Dirk, ed. *The Greek New Testament, Produced by Tyndale House, Cambridge*. Wheaton: Crossway, 2017.

Köstenberger, Andreas J., Benjamin L. Merkle, and Robert L. Plummer. *Going Deeper with New Testament Greek: An Intermediate Study of the Grammar and Syntax of the New Testament*. Nashville: B&H Academic, 2016.

Levinsohn, Stephen H. *Discourse Features of New Testament Greek: A Coursebook*. 2nd ed. Dallas: Summer Institute of Linguistics, 2000.

Levinson, Stephen C. *Pragmatics*. Cambridge Textbooks in Linguistics. Cambridge: Cambridge University Press, 1983.

Long, Fredrick J. *Koine Greek Grammar: A Beginning-Intermediate Exegetical and Pragmatic Handbook*. Wilmore: GlossaHouse, 2015.

Long, Gary A. *Grammatical Concepts 101 for Biblical Greek*. Peabody: Hendrickson, 2006.

Louw, J. P. "On Greek Prohibitions." *Acta Classica* 2 (1959): 43–57.

Lyons, John. *Introduction to Theoretical Linguistics*. Cambridge: Cambridge University Press, 1969.

———. *Semantics*. Vol. 2. Cambridge: Cambridge University Press, 1977.

Mangum, Douglas, and Josh Westbury, eds. *Linguistics and Biblical Exegesis*. Bellingham, WA: Lexham Press, 2017.

Martín-Asensio, Gustavo. *Transitivity-Based Foregrounding in the Acts of the Apostles: A Functional-Grammatical Approach to the Lukan Perspective*. Journal for the Study of the New Testament Supplement Series 202. Sheffield: Sheffield Academic, 2000.

Mathewson, David L. *Revelation: A Handbook on the Greek Text*. Waco: Baylor University Press, 2016.

———. "Verbal Aspect in Imperatival Constructions in Pauline Ethical Injunctions." *Filología Neotestamentaria* 9 (1996): 21–35.

Mathewson, David L., and Elodie Ballantine Emig. *Intermediate Greek Grammar: Syntax for Students of the New Testament*. Grand Rapids: Baker Academic, 2016.

McKay, Kenneth L. "Aspect in Imperatival Constructions in New Testament Greek." *Novum Testamentum* 27 (1985): 201–26.

———. *A New Syntax of the Verb in New Testament Greek: An Aspectual Approach*. Studies in Biblical Greek 5. New York: Peter Lang, 1994.

Moule, C. F. D. *An Idiom Book of New Testament Greek*. 2nd ed. Cambridge: Cambridge University Press, 1959.

Nestle, Eberhard, Erwin Nestle, Barbara Aland, Kurt Aland, Johannes Karavidopoulos, Carlo M. Martini, and Bruce M. Metzger, eds. *Novum Testamentum Graece*. 28th rev. ed. Stuttgart: Deutsche Bibelgesellschaft, 2012.

Novakovic, Lidija. *Philippians: A Handbook on the Greek Text*. Waco: Baylor, 2020.

O'Donnell, Matthew Brook. *Corpus Linguistics and the Greek New Testament*. New Testament Monographs 6. Sheffield: Sheffield Phoenix, 2005.

———. "Some New Testament Words of Resurrection and the Company They Keep." In *Resurrection*, edited by Stanley E. Porter, Michael A. Hayes, and David Tombs, 136–63. Journal for the Study of the New Testament Supplement Series 186. Sheffield: Sheffield Academic, 1999.

Palmer, F. R. *Mood and Modality*. 2nd ed. Cambridge Textbooks in Linguistics. Cambridge: Cambridge University Press, 2001.

Pennington, Jonathan T. "Setting Aside 'Deponency': Rediscovering the Greek Middle Voice in New Testament Studies." In *The Linguist as Peda-*

gogue: Trends in the Teaching and Linguistic Analysis of the Greek New Testament, edited by Stanley E. Porter and Matthew Brook O'Donnell, 181–203. Sheffield: Sheffield Phoenix, 2009.

Peters, Ronald D. *The Greek Article: A Functional Grammar of O-Items in the Greek New Testament with Special Emphasis on the Greek Article.* Linguistic Biblical Studies 9. Leiden: Brill, 2014.

Porter, Stanley E. "Aspect and Imperatives Once More." *Biblical and Ancient Greek Linguistics* 7 (2018): 141–72.

———. "Did Paul Baptize Himself? A Problem in the Greek Voice System." In *Dimensions of Baptism: Biblical and Theological Studies*, edited by S. E. Porter and A. R. Cross, 91–109. Journal for the Study of the New Testament Supplement Series 234. Sheffield: Sheffield Academic, 2002.

———. *Idioms of the Greek New Testament.* Sheffield: JSOT Press, 1992.

———. *Linguistic Analysis of the Greek New Testament: Studies in Tools, Methods, and Practice.* Grand Rapids: Baker Academic, 2015.

———. "Prominence: An Overview." In *The Linguist as Pedagogue: Trends in Teaching and Linguistic Analysis of the Greek New Testament*, edited by Stanley E. Porter and Matthew Brook O'Donnell, 45–74. Sheffield: Sheffield Phoenix, 2009.

———. "Systemic Functional Linguistics and the Greek Language: The Need for Further Modeling." In *Modeling Biblical Language: Select Papers from the McMaster Divinity College Linguistics Circle*, edited by Stanley E. Porter, Gregory P. Fewster, and Christopher D. Land, 9–47. Linguistic Biblical Studies 13. Leiden: Brill, 2016.

———. "Vague Verbs, Periphrastics, and Matt 16.19." *Filología Neotestamentaria* 1 (1988): 155–73.

———. *Verbal Aspect in the Greek of the New Testament, with Reference to Tense and Mood.* Studies in Biblical Greek 1. New York: Peter Lang, 1989.

Porter, Stanley E., and Matthew Brook O'Donnell. "The Greek Verbal System Viewed from a Probabalistic Standpoint." *Filología Neotestamentaria* 14 (2001): 3–41.

Reed, Jeffrey T. *Discourse Analysis of Philippians: Method and Rhetoric in the Debate over Literary Integrity.* Journal for the Study of the New Testament Supplement Series 136. Sheffield: Sheffield Academic, 1997.

———. "The Infinitive with Two Accusative Substantives: An Ambiguous Construction." *Novum Testamentum* 33 (1991): 1–27.

Rijksbaron, Albert. *The Syntax and Semantics of the Verb in Classical Greek: An Introduction*. 3rd ed. Chicago: University of Chicago Press, 2002.

Robertson, A. T. *A Grammar of the Greek New Testament in the Light of Historical Research*. Nashville: Broadman, 1934.

Robertson, A. T., and W. Hersey Davis. *A New Short Grammar of the Greek Testament*. 10th ed. Grand Rapids: Baker, 1977.

Runge, Steven E. *Discourse Grammar of the Greek New Testament: A Practical Introduction for Teaching and Exegesis*. Peabody, MA: Hendrickson, 2010.

Silzer, Peter James, and Thomas John Finley. *How Biblical Languages Work: A Student's Guide to Learning Greek and Hebrew*. Grand Rapids: Kregel Academic, 2004.

Tan, Randall. "Prominence in the Pauline Letters." In *The Linguist as Pedagogue: Trends in Teaching and Linguistic Analysis of the Greek New Testament*, edited by Stanley E. Porter and Matthew Brook O'Donnell, 93–110. Sheffield: Sheffield Phoenix, 2009.

Taylor, Bernard A. "Deponency and Greek Lexicography." In *Biblical Greek Language and Lexicography*, edited by Bernard A. Taylor, John A. L. Lee, Peter R. Burton, and Richard E. Whitaker, 167–76. Grand Rapids: Eerdmans, 2004.

Thompson, Geoff. *Introducing Functional Grammar*. 2nd ed. London: Hodder, 2004.

Thompson, Geoff, Wendy L. Bowcher, Lise Fontaine, and David Schönthal, eds. *The Cambridge Handbook of Systemic Functional Linguistics*. Cambridge: Cambridge University Press, 2019.

Turner, Nigel. *Syntax*. Vol. 3 of *Grammar of New Testament Greek*. Edinburgh: T&T Clark, 1963.

van Emde Boas, Evert, Albert Rijksbaron, Luuk Huitink, and Mathieu de Bakker. *The Cambridge Grammar of Classical Greek*. Cambridge: Cambridge University Press, 2019.

Vlachos, Chris A. *James: Exegetical Guide to the Greek New Testament*. Nashville: Broadman & Holman, 2013.

von Siebenthal, Heinrich. *Ancient Greek Grammar for the Study of the New Testament*. Oxford: Peter Lang, 2019.

Wallace, Daniel B. *Greek Grammar Beyond the Basics: An Exegetical Syntax of the New Testament*. Grand Rapids: Zondervan, 1996.

Westfall, Cynthia. *A Discourse Analysis of the Letter to the Hebrews: The Relationship Between Form and Meaning.* Library of New Testament Studies 297. London: T&T Clark, 2005.

Yoon, David L. *A Discourse Analysis of Galatians and the New Perspective on Paul.* Linguistic Biblical Studies 17. Leiden: Brill, 2019.

Young, Richard A. *Intermediate New Testament Greek: A Linguistic and Exegetical Approach.* Nashville: Broadman & Holman, 1994.

Zúñiga, Fernando, and Seppo Kittilä. *Grammatical Voice.* Cambridge Textbooks in Linguistics. Cambridge: Cambridge University Press, 2019.

AUTHOR INDEX

Adam, M. A. K., 72

Allan, Rutger J., 16–18, 19, 20, 22, 45, 47, 57

Aubrey, Rachel, 18–20, 22, 45, 46n54, 47, 59

Berry, Margaret, 93n54

Black, David Alan, 12, 71n32, 83, 84n23, 152n23, 155

Blass, Friedrich, 154n25

Boas, Van Emde, 41n43

Boyer, James, 79n3, 106

Callow, Kathleen, 130n66

Campbell, Constantine R., 15n27, 70n28, 71, 128n63

Carson, D. A., 39n40, 68n26, 106n24

Clackson, James, 64n20

Culy, Martin M., 62n17

Dana, H. E., 71n32, 154n25

Davis, W. Hersey, 106n23

Debrunner, Albert, 154n25

Decker, Rodney J., 1n1

Dixon, R. M. W., 30, 34n30

Donovan, J., 128n62

Dubis, Mark, 58n11, 161n49

Dvorak, James, 77, 79n3, 123, 127

Emig, Elodie Ballantine, 2n3, 4n8, 13, 32, 56n5, 57n9, 62n17, 64n19, 68n26, 84–85, 88, 89n35, 101n17, 105n22, 106n24, 106n25, 110n31, 112n32, 116n37, 121n45, 126n59, 131n67, 131n70, 137n2, 142n14, 143n15, 147n19, 153n24, 157, 159n47, 162n53, 165n58

Evans, Vyvyan, 90n43, 91n45, 91n47

Fanning, Buist M., 128n63

Fantin, Joseph R., 79n3, 122–23

Fletcher, Bryan W. Y., 8n1, 18n32, 20–22, 32, 33, 35, 36n35, 39n39, 45, 46n52, 47, 48n61, 49n62, 51n1, 53n2, 57n50, 66

Friberg, Barbara, 70n31

Friberg, Timothy, 70n31

Gonda, J., 100, 109, 110, 117

Halliday, M. A. K., 20, 21, 25, 26, 27, 28, 29, 30, 31, 32, 37, 38, 39,

42n48, 44n49, 44n50, 49, 66, 91, 92, 93, 94, 98, 99, 134n73
Harris, Dana, 15n27, 70n28
Hopper, Paul J., 56n4
Huffman, Douglas S., 128n64

Jongkind, Dirk, 58n10

Kittilä, Seppo, 43n48, 56n6, 62n18
Köstenberger, Andreas J., 9n2, 12, 84, 152n23

Levinsohn, Steven H., 158n45, 162n53
Long, Gary A., 126n58
Louw, J. P., 128n62
Lyons, John, 8n1, 30n21, 42n47, 88n34, 91n44, 91n46

Mantey, Julius R., 71n32, 154n25
Martín-Asensio, Gustavo, 26n2, 28n14
Mathewson, David L., 2n3, 4n8, 13, 32, 56n5, 57n9, 62n17, 64n19, 68n26, 69n27, 84–85, 88, 89n35, 101n17, 105n22, 106n24, 106n25, 110n31, 112n32, 115n35, 116n37, 121n45, 126n59, 127n61, 128n64, 131n67, 131n70, 132n72, 137n2, 142n14, 143n15, 147n17, 147n19, 153n24, 157, 159n47, 161n50, 162n53, 165n58
Matthiessen, Christian M. I. M., 29n15, 29n17, 29n18, 30n19, 43n48, 66n23, 92n52, 92n53
McKay, Kenneth L., 10, 11, 59n12, 64n19, 81–82, 128n64, 131, 157
Merkle, Benjamin L., 9n2, 12, 84, 152n23
Moule, C. F. D., 112n32

Novakovic, Lidija, 141n12

O'Donnell, Matthew Brook, 2n5, 15n27, 33, 35, 36n34, 38, 39n39, 48n60, 60n15, 65n22

Palmer, F. R., 90, 91n44, 91n46, 91n48, 95n1, 95n2, 100n14, 101n16, 109n28, 122, 138
Pennington, Jonathan T., 71n33, 71n35
Peters, Ronald D., 26n2
Plummer, Robert L., 9n2, 12, 84, 152n23
Porter, Stanley E., 2n5, 4n7, 9, 10, 11, 15n27, 26n2, 26n5, 27, 32n24, 33, 34, 35n33, 36n34, 38, 39n40, 40, 45n51, 46n53, 57n9, 64, 65n22, 70n29, 77, 79, 80–81, 88, 89n35, 92n51, 93, 94, 95n1, 96, 98, 99, 101, 103, 106n23, 108n26, 110, 111, 112n32, 117, 118n42, 119n44, 124, 127n61, 128n64, 131, 132n71, 137n1, 137n2, 138, 139n8, 141n10, 141n11, 142n13, 144n16, 150n20, 150n21, 151, 155, 156, 157, 159n47, 160n48, 161n51, 163n54, 163n56, 165n57, 166n60

Reed, Jeffrey T., 26n2, 98, 99, 134n74, 141n11
Rijksbaron, Albert, 39
Robertson, A. T., 2n4, 42, 70, 106n23
Runge, Steven E., 158n46

Tan, Randall, 26n6
Taylor, Bernard A., 47n59, 71n34, 71n35
Thompson, Geoff, 25n1, 29n15
Thompson, Sandra A., 56n4
Turner, Nigel, 154n25

Vlachos, Chris A., 72n36
von Siebenthal, Heinrich, 13, 32,
    33n25, 86, 87n32, 87n33, 88,
    90n38, 91n49, 100, 124n57,
    126n59, 137n2, 138, 140n9,
    141n10, 142n13, 147n18,
    147n19, 155, 163

Wallace, Daniel B., 4n8, 9n2, 11,
    12n18, 14n26, 33n25, 39n40,
    42n44, 42n46, 57n9, 64n19,
    82–83, 88, 89, 114n33, 118,
    121n46, 122n50, 128n63, 137n2,

141n10, 141n11, 152n23, 155,
    156, 166n63
Westfall, Cynthia, 26n2, 116n36

Yoon, David L., 26n2
Young, Richard, 10, 39n37, 64n19,
    71n32, 80, 81, 152n23, 155,
    158n44, 161, 162n53, 166n61,
    166n62, 166n63

Zúñiga, Fernando, 43n48, 56n6,
    62n18

SCRIPTURE INDEX

Matthew

1:18–19 60
1:20 48, 60, 112
1:21 134
1:22 57
2:2 146
2:11 158
2:13 69, 146, 162
2:15 113
4 114
4:3 115
4:6 115
4:9 114
5:17 140
5:23 43
5:25 166
5:28 148
6:18 153
6:27 104
6:31 113
7:1 125
7:7–11 72n36
8:1 161, 162
11:1 166
12 106
12:2 142
12:23 103
12:27–28 107
13:4 148
14:18 129
14:28 48
15:25 127
16:13 144
16:19 165
18:18 165
24:9 164
27:20 53
27:24 66
28:19–20 158

Mark

1:9 63
1:12 44
1:13 41
1:14 148
3:29 114
5:1–8 108
9:29 144
10:14 143
11:14 118
12:14 112

Luke

1:24 54
1:29 119
2:5 67
2:30 43
3:15 120
4:4 134
4:7 115n34
4:35 125
7:29 62
9:57 133
11:29 162
12:4 167
15:19 145
15:26 120
24:45 146

John

3:1–15 48
3:3–6 129
3:7 129
3:16 69
4:10 54
4:49 148
6:28 113

7:21 102
7:42 105
17:5 148

Acts

1:11 133
1:16 144
2:3 60
2:16–21 60
2:17 60
3:19 140
5:42 166
7:40 105
7:58 66
8:20 118
8:40 147n19
10:44 162
11:19 153
17:18 120
21:33 120
24:19 121

Romans

1:13 144
3:23 43
5:1 58
5:11 161
6:1–2 119, 131
6:2 117, 121
6:3 104
6:6 141
6:11 145
6:12 125, 148
6:12–13 131
6:12–15 130
6:13 130
6:15 112, 117, 119,
   121
7:3 132
8:5 167

12:9 161
12:10–19 161
12:14 150
12:14–15 151
12:15 150

1 Corinthians

2:6 53
2:8 108
7:12 130
10:31 125
12 68
13:8 39, 68, 69
14:7 133
14:9 133
15:3 61, 102
15:4 61
15:12 107

2 Corinthians

1:8 146
1:9 165
7:12 147n19
8:11 143, 147n19

Galatians

1:1 55
1:14 55
1:22 164
3:2 103
3:14 113
5:16 112, 116

Ephesians

1–3 130, 135
1:4 67
2:5 164
2:8 164
2:20 162
4–6 130, 135

4:26 126
5:19–21 156

Philippians

1:7 141, 149
1:21 142

Colossians

1:6 69
1:9 62, 166
2:6–7 159
2:13–15 108
2:16–19 108
3:4 114

1 Thessalonians

4:13 154

2 Thessalonians

3:16 119

1 Timothy

2:11 125

2 Timothy

2:4 159

Titus

3:4 105

Hebrews

1:3 160
2:8 149
2:15 147n19
4:11 116
4:11–16 116
4:12–13 116
4:14 116
4:16 116

James

1:1 150
1:4 165n59
1:19 126
1:22 125
1:27 145
2:6 103
2:13 167
4:2 68, 72, 149
4:2–3 68, 72
4:3 72
4:15 147n19

1 Peter

1:3 154
1:13 67
1:14 161
2:18 161
3:14 121
3:17 121
4:1 163

4:7 55
4:11 58

1 John

2:15 115
2:22 167
3:7 53
5:1 167
5:21 129

Jude

3 61

Revelation

1:7 69
1:18 164
2:5 115
2:5–7 115
2:10 144
3:8 130

3:9 132, 145
3:10 105, 130
3:11 130
5:4 39, 40n41
5:5 125, 147
5:14 55
7:4 167
7:13 160
11:7 133
11:8 61
11:18 67
13:5 146
14:4 114
16:9 62
17:4 164
18:5 54
19:7 54, 112
19:21 58, 154
20:3 143
21:14 161
22:20 127

SUBJECT INDEX

active voice, 52–56
  meaning, 52–53
  in intransitive clauses, 54–55
  in transitive clauses, 53–54
agency, 36
agent
  external. *See* passive voice
  subject as direct, 36, 52–53
Allan, Rutger J., 15–18
Aubrey, Rachel, 18–20

Black, David Alan, 12, 83–84

causality, 33–36, 38
  direct, 36–38
  external, 36–38, 57
  internal. *See* middle voice:
    meaning

deontic modality, 90–91
deponency, 15, 70–71, 170
  critique of, 71
  middle only, 71, 170
Dvorak, James, 123

Emig, Elodie Ballantine, 13, 84–86
epistemic modality, 90–91, 100
ergativity, 29–32

Fantin, Joseph R., 122–23
Fletcher, Bryan M. Y., 20–23
future tense form, 131
  command, 134
  deliberative, 133
  meaning, 131
  prospective, 133
  and relation to mood, 132–33

Gonda, J., 100, 109, 110

Halliday, H. A. K., 25–32, 91–94

imperative mood, 122
  in commands, 125
  meaning, 124–25
  in prohibitions, 125
  in requests, 126–27
  in the third person, 126
  with verbal aspect, 127–30
indicative mood, 100–101
  in assertion, 100
  in conditional clauses, 105–8
  in declarative statements, 102
  in embedded clauses, 105
  in questions, 102–4
  in secondary clauses, 105

infinitives, 137–38, 139–40
  as adverbial adjuncts, 146–47
  meaning, 140
  and modifiers, noun/adjective,
    145–46
  and participles, semantic distinc-
    tion from, 138–39
  as predicates, 149–50
  with prepositions, 147–49
  subject of, 140–41
  as substantives, 142–45
intransitivity, 42–43

Köstenberger, Andreas J., 12, 84

Mathewson, David L., 13, 84–86
McKay, Kenneth L., 10–11, 81–82
meaning and choice, 2, 26
medium, 21, 30–36
Merkle, Benjamin L., 12, 84
middle voice, 57, 63–65
  as deponent. See deponency
  and ergativity. See middle voice:
    meaning
  in intransitive clauses, 67–69
  meaning, 36–38, 64–65
  range, 65–66
  in transitive clauses, 65–67
modality, epistemic, 90–91, 100
mood, 3–4, 77–79, 96
  assertive vs. nonassertive, 96
  definition, 3, 88–89
  nonassertive, 109
  and reality, 89, 90, 95
  statistics for, 101
  See also individual moods

O'Donnell, Matthew Brook, 35
optative mood, 116–17
  in contingent questions, 119–20
  in contingent statements, 118

  meaning, 117
  in secondary clauses, 120–21

participles, 137–38, 151–53
  and the article, importance of,
    152–53
  and the genitive absolute, 161–63
  as independent verb, 160–61
  and the infinitive, semantic dis-
    tinction from, 138–39
  meaning, 151
  and modifiers
    adverbial, 154–60
    attributive, 153
    functions of adverbial, 157–58
  periphrastic, 163–66
    distinction from finite verbs,
      163–64
  substantive, 166–68
  supplementary, 166
passive voice, 56–57
  with accusative noun, 62
  and external agency, 57–59
  meaning, 56–57
  as not reflexive, 63–64
  and -(θ)η- ending, 17–19, 46,
    47–49, 59
  and unexpressed agency, 59–61
patient, the, 56
perspective, 39
Plummer, Robert R., 12, 84
Porter, Stanley E., 9–10, 79–80,
  96–98, 110

speech roles, 92–93
  in English, 92–93
  and the Greek mood, 97–100
subject, 33–34
  affectedness, 15, 64
  as agent. See agent
  as medium. See medium

subjunctive mood, 109–11
  in conditionals, 114–15
  meaning, 110
  in questions, 112–13
  in secondary clauses, 113–15
  in statements, 111–12
Systemic Functional Linguistics,
    25–32, 91–93
  and metafunctions of language, 27

transitivity, 27–28, 33–34, 42–43
  relationship to voice, 44–45

voice(s), 2–3, 51–52
  definition, 2, 32–33, 40
  morphology of, 40–42
  number of, 45–46
  statistics for, 52
  See also individual voices
von Siebenthal, Heinrich, 13–14,
    86–87

Wallace, Daniel B., 11–12, 82–83, 89

Young, Richard, 10, 80–81